Praise for Return to OZ

This two part book compares the perceptions of a displaced teenager and a world wise traveller. John Brown's honest and inspiring view of the people and places he is visiting would make an excellent read for your next long flight Down Under. This honest and humorous account of life in Australia now and then – is sure to bring a smile to your face.
Kelly Marie Dudley
AUSTRALIA & NZ MAGAZINE

Return to Oz by John Brown, is one book but has two parts. Part one describes what it was like to land in Australia as a 'Ten Pound Pom'. The second part is a direct, up to date comparison.
John Brown has a wicked eye for the absurd and his work is obviously researched as well as funny. I would recommend this book to anyone about to visit Oz, or anybody who just loves a good travel read – if you like Tim Moore or Bill Bryson then you'll love this.
BBC Collective
TRAVEL IN OZ!

A cathartic journey of rediscovery. It made me laugh, it nearly made me cry and it definitely made me want to catch the next plane for Oz.
Peter Knight
PETER KNIGHT ASSOCIATES

NORTH
OF
WATFORD GAP

... a close-up view of "the North"

SilverWood

Other titles by this author
The Original Teds
Return to Oz
Which Way Next ?

For more information and photos of the places featured within this book please visit www.northofwatfordgap.co.uk

Published in paperback by SilverWood Books 2010
www.silverwoodbooks.co.uk

ISBN 978-1-906236-31-1

British Library Cataloguing in Publication Data
A CIP catalogue record for this book is available from the British Library

Set in 11pt Adobe Garamond Pro by SilverWood Books
Printed in England by Cpod, Trowbridge

World rights: Peter Knight Book Associates, London

*Dedicated to all you artisans:
keep pushing the boundaries*

Contents

Introduction

When I first thought of writing about the UK I envisaged it would encompass the complete British Isles. However, the more I thought about the project, the more the truth dawned that this book should be about the counties north of Watford Gap. I have no wish to exclude large parts of the UK on the grounds of some prejudicial dislike. Quite the contrary, I spent a good deal of my formative years with Nipper the Dog at the Hayes headquarters of EMI music, and my literary agent is based in London. My daughter lives in the beautiful county of Hampshire, as does a good friend. I have also been known to motor down to deepest Cornwall or Sussex. So you see, I'm not unacquainted with the South, which is more than can be said for a charming lady I met recently whilst on holiday in the town of Kalkan, Turkey. At a guess she was probably in her late forties, and openly admitted with a somewhat squeaky giggle that 'the furthest she had ever ventured from her home in Hampstead was Wimbledon, for the tennis of course'.

I was gob-smacked. She had visited half the countries of the world, cruised the Aegean Sea, travelled across the USA... but never been north of Watford Gap. The Lake District was just a blur on her radar and Wales some distant land with choirs and miners. Whilst Manchester – well, that was for the pioneer corps. Her husband, it's fair to say, had a better grasp of places north of Wimbledon. Originally from Leeds, he was fully aware that the M1 Motorway had a beginning, a middle and, strangely enough, an end. If we listened to the daily outpouring from our media, we as a country are crushed, battered and all but a busted flush. As for 'the North', that's just so far beyond redemption it doesn't even merit airtime. To certain sectors of the populace domiciled in Chelsea or one of the chocolate-box pretty, villages that nestle comfortably along the meandering Thames, the North still conjures up images of whippets and clogs, *Coronation Street* and mills, black pudding and tripe. A place where half the population is unemployed, and therefore supported by the honest endeavours of those who daily toil in the city. Not to mention the shoeless, malnourished urchins commonly found upon any street corner.

The recent worldwide recession has done nothing to rectify this image, but in truth, the real 'North' is a million miles away from this distortion. It is as complex and ever changing as any part of the British Isles, a veritable melting pot of cultures and diverse beliefs, equally complex whether you reside in the North or South. It is a place of serious wealth as witnessed in the areas south of Manchester, where footballers and businessmen build ever larger properties in an odd game of one-upmanship. Whilst on sink estates, less than twenty miles away, people struggle to make sense of their dispiriting and often violent communities. It is a region where Lakeland Fells, immortalized by Alfred Wainwright, have no equal, and disturbingly pretty villages and hamlets pop up with alarming regularity. It is a place where moorland hillsides sit proudly against threatening leaden skies; a place where coastal walks lift the spirit, and sites such as Holy Island dramatically appear across a wide inviting sand bank. Shall I go on? The picture-perfect villages of North Yorkshire, the wistful Brontë country, the elegant spa towns of Harrogate and Buxton, the energy of great cities such as Newcastle and Liverpool, not to mention the sheer prettiness of Cheshire and the serine Trough of Bowland – these are but small snapshots of the real 'North'.

* * *

In taking a more in-depth look at places north of Watford Gap, there seemed no more perfect place to start my journey than my hometown (city actually) of Manchester. Although not exactly in the centre of the UK, it is within easy reach of twenty or more important cities and landmarks. The motorway network is excellent, whilst the train equally services almost every point of the compass. I would not use any one particular mode of transport in my quest for a snapshot of this area, but simply adopt the best route as I went along. What itinerary there would be would radiate out from the city and then progress in an anticlockwise transit, or something of that nature.

Well, that's the plan, how it pans out may be something entirely different.

Manchester

It was Saturday 15th June 1996 (Father's Day) when a 3,000lb IRA bomb exploded in Manchester. The blast injured more than two hundred people and ripped into the fabric of the city's main shopping area. Thanks to several coded warnings to newspapers and radio stations, police had already begun clearing the suspected area some forty minutes before the blast. Unbelievably no one was killed. The nearest thing to a fatality had occurred before the actual explosion, when a rather zealous parking attendant had placed a fixed penalty notice upon the screen of the explosive-laden truck. I suspect this person is still in therapy. Shortly after this momentous event in Manchester's varied history, Bill Bryson launched his bestselling book *Notes From A Small Island* on an unsuspecting British public, setting the tone for many future travel writers with his irreverent style. We no longer had to view travel writing through the eyes of a dowdy geography teacher on some school field trip. I, along with countless others, enjoyed Bill's light-hearted romp through his adopted homeland. The appeal of his work being that despite his obvious American upbringing, he was more English in his outlook and attitude than most residents. This allowed him to appraise our island with an independent but kindly eye. The one blot on his otherwise critically acclaimed work came when he visited pre-blast Manchester. To say he was a little disparaging would be an understatement; he was withering in his comments about my city.

A decade or so later Bill returned, his demeanour a little more conciliatory, in fact, almost glowing in his praise of 'the New Manchester.' I have to declare here and now, I am a proud Mancunian and Bill definitely missed the real Manchester on his first visit.

Manchester has always been unique. What was no more than a sleepy village in the early 18th century grew at an alarming rate to conquer the world. Between 1760 and 1790, Richard Arkwright had invented the Water Frame, and Samuel Crompton the Spinning Mule, revolutionising the production of cotton. Meanwhile, good turnpike roads were improving communications, and the Earl of Bridgewater was busy building the canal that bears his name. Huge quantities of cheap coal could now be brought directly into the heart of Manchester, perfect for the 1783 opening of the first steam-powered mill. The importation of raw cotton had soared from 1000 tonnes in 1751, to a staggering 45.2 thousand tonnes by 1816. Manchester had arrived.

Ironbridge in Shropshire rightly lays claim to being the birthplace of the industrial revolution. Without its iron, none of our great cities would have sprung forth to establish themselves in such an impressive way. Leeds, Liverpool, Sheffield, Birmingham, etc, all took advantage of the new technology emanating from this bedrock of industry in Salop. Whilst the men at Ironbridge forged the way (sorry), it was the foresight and pure business acumen of several notable Mancunians who recognized the huge opportunities offered by the cotton trade. The word Manchester rapidly became synonymous with the cotton industry. Importing the raw commodity, then re-exporting the finished fabric to all corners of the globe, gave this city the nickname of 'King Cotton,' and its wealthy mill owners became the 'barons of Cottonopolis'.

It didn't take long for me to realise that like certain people in the South, I too was guilty of ignoring some of the finer points of this historic city. They had an excuse; they lived a railway journey away. I on the other hand had no excuses. I lived a mere half hour's distance from the centre of the city. Oh sure, I had passed the statues and glanced at the odd building on my frequent visits to Manchester, but not until this moment had I truly recognized or appreciated the wealth of culture and history that lay before me.

The list of famous Mancunians is long, diverse, and impressive. Among such worthy souls are the first women's libbers Emmeline and Christabel Pankhurst; the statesman Lloyd George (yes, Lloyd George); the artist L.S. Lowry; the architect Sir Norman Foster; the Pre-Raphelite painter Ford Madox Brown; the actors Ben Kingsley, Robert Powell and John Thaw; Sir Humphrey Chetham, founder of the world-famous school of music; at least thirteen holders of the Victoria Cross and more famous sportsman and musicians than can be listed in this short appraisal.

Oxford Road today is a hectic, bus-strewn route leading to the city centre. I walked a good deal of its length in the opposite direction in a vain attempt to find Nelson Street and the former home of Emmeline Pankhurst. The passers-by on this bright December morning in Manchester seemed blissfully unaware of the mere existence of this historic figure, much less the whereabouts of her former abode.

"Excuse me, am I anywhere near the Emmeline Pankhurst house?" I asked a young student.

"Emily who? What does she do?"

"She doesn't do anything now, she's dead." I realised the futility of my question almost as soon as I asked it

"Sorry mate, can't help ya."

Don't you just love being called 'mate'?

My second attempt at directional help was via a pretty, sallow-skinned teenager, her appearance made even more arresting by the multi-coloured necklace she wore, which had all the hallmarks of a Rio Carnival frontispiece.

"Excuse me, I'm looking for the Emmeline Pankhurst house, can you help me?"

"Oh yeah, the house what the suvrajet lived at init? Down there on the left about half a mile init."

I was fascinated by her abstract use of English. I first came across the word 'init' used as a suffix to almost every sentence whilst on a bus journey through Brixton a couple of years ago. Cast your mind back to a February day when the wind was ripping up roof tiles and scattering them like playing cards. Huge sections of the underground were out of action and my only means of transport from Clapham Common to London Central was via the big red bus. For a good deal of the journey (a never ending two hours) I was the only 'white guy on the bus', a fascinating situation, made all the more so by the use of this strange patois. All of the passengers from approximately twelve to thirty years of age liberally sprinkled their conversations with 'init'. I'd always thought that life was imitating art when I first heard these fractured sentences, but this time it was definitely the other way round. Listening to it in this odd situation seemed strangely normal.

I followed the directions from the 'init girl' and sure enough, there at the end of Nelson Street stood the one-time home of Emmeline Pankhurst. Any resemblance to the small tree-lined avenue that this obviously once was, has long since disappeared. Surrounded on all sides by the various buildings that go to make up Manchester Royal Infirmary, it sits like a dwarfed minnow. From this modest red brick, double-fronted house at No 62 Nelson Street, Pankhurst first set out her plans for the Women's Suffrage Movement. It was intriguing to think that from this residence, this single-minded lady laid the cornerstone for the most important piece of twentieth century legislation, its effect touching every modern-day female in the country.

I rang the bell and was greeted by one of the custodians of the Pankhurst Centre. This kindly lady showed me the various articles and artifacts that adorn the hallway and one of the inner rooms. We then proceeded to 'Emily's sitting room'. The room was compact (approximately twelve foot by eleven), with full height, Gothic-style windows and doors that opened on to a small side garden. On a neat table in one corner of the room sat a black Underwood typewriter. This was the actual machine that Emmeline used to type out the basic newssheets for her propaganda. Even more surreal were the sashes of purple and green on a white background, the official colours of the sufferance movement (and strangely reminiscent of the Wimbledon tennis colours), loosely draped over a chair. Sashes like these had been worn by Emmeline, her daughters, and her many followers to their countless rallies over the most tempestuous years of their struggle.

Left to absorb the atmosphere of this home, and this room in particular, I felt a positive sense of the magnitude of their task. Looking from a twenty-first century perspective it is hard to imagine the prejudice of their age, and the intransigence of the post-Victorian politicians. My friendly lady returned and promptly sat me down and invited me to watch a fifteen-minute video of the original occupant and her fellow protestors. Watching this rare footage of these remarkable ladies, and ladies they certainly were, I was struck by how many of them were so obviously middle-class. Unlike their 1960s counterparts, there would be no bra-burning from these girls! They were well-dressed, impeccably groomed, and many of them obviously happily married. Their quest was not to crush men or ridicule them, but simply to obtain full voting rights for all women. The video ended with a haunting portrait of Emmeline Pankhurst, complete with the diagonally placed sash across her blouse. Here I was in the great lady's former sitting room, viewing her haunting image – very odd. Unlike many places of historical interest, where things feel somehow frozen in aspic, the Pankhurst Centre, as it is now known, is currently used as a women's drop-in centre, the upstairs rooms and the adjoining house hosting a range of self-help classes and advice. I think Emmeline would approve.

Having reduced my shoe leather to some degree in pursuit of Emmeline, I decided my trip back into central Manchester would be via the big red bus (it was actually the blue, orange and white of Stagecoach). Sitting on the front seat of the upper deck like an over-excited six year old, I viewed the changing scene below me. For the full length of the University of Manchester buildings, students walked four and five abreast, many of them making their way to graduation ceremonies. With their flowing gowns and mortar-boards in hand they happily sauntered along in the bright morning sunshine. How many of the young ladies among them, I wondered, realised the debt of gratitude they owed to the lady in Nelson Street?

Stand in Albert Square, Manchester and the all-encompassing view that surrounds you is that of the magnificent Neo-Gothic Town Hall. It simply dwarfs all other buildings within the immediate area, both in grandeur and sheer ornamentation. Designed by the architect Alfred Waterhouse and built between 1868-77, it is now a Grade One listed building. The frontage belies the awkwardness of the original site (an irregular triangle), but Waterhouse, more commonly known for his work on London's Natural History Museum, shoe-horned in all his client's requirements with consummate skill. The structure comprises some fourteen million bricks encased in Spinkwell stone and came complete with a revolutionary warm-air heating system.

You may have seen this great building and not even known you were viewing it. The arched ceilings and wide sweeping staircases of the Manchester Town Hall doubled for the interior of the House of Commons in the TV series *House of Cards*, featuring the late Ian Richardson as the evil P.M. Francis Urquhart. A wise choice of location, for not only was the Town Hall the perfect setting for the Palace of Westminster, but down the road at Granada studios was the most authentic replica of the green, leather-lined benches of the House of Commons, complete with the huge Speaker's Chair.

My visit to this remarkable building was less threatening than the aforementioned actor's; my purpose in climbing the wide staircase that leads to the central meeting room was to view the 'Great Hall'.

I donned the lapel badge, obligatory for all visitors wishing to venture any further than the ground floor, and proceeded up the grand staircase. At the head of the staircase, a wide gallery has several huge double doors leading to the various reception rooms. I had received instructions that 'as long as the door to each room is open you can wander freely.' The fact that no other person crossed my radar was doubly satisfying.

The 'Great Hall' is exactly that. A huge barrel-vaulted ceiling is sectioned into twenty-eight distinct panels, each depicting the heraldic shield of a country or British city. Here Russia mingles with Leeds and Denmark with Liverpool. High up the wall on either side of the doorway, white parion busts of Victoria and Albert look censoriously down onto the mere mortals below. The Town Hall's gem, though, has to be the twelve wall murals painted by the Pre-Raphelite artist Ford Madox Brown. They are a must for anybody who appreciates the muted colours and illusory quality of this period of art, unique in their representation of industrial Empire, whilst possessing a dream-like quality. Directly opposite the hall sits the Mayor's Parlour, complete with ante room, which in turn links to two humungous banqueting suites. This is a town hall built at a time when Manchester held tremendous prestige and was a huge player in world terms, a position the city fathers were determined to reinforce at every opportunity.

Looking out from the Mayor's parlour, I was greeted with an arial view of the festive market. For the past decade the huge cobbled area that fronts the Town Hall (Albert Square) has played host to the Christmas market. Predominantly German in origin, the various stalls display a wide array of continental goods. From my exalted viewpoint, the all-pervading aroma was one of gluvine and bratwurst, intoxicating stuff, even for a Lord Mayor. I said goodbye to Gladstone, or at least his life size statue, within the Town Hall Foyer and rejoined the happy Mancunians, by now replete from their continental indulgencies.

The newly named district of Spinningfield's is principally a collection of high-tech glass-fronted buildings in a variety of shapes and colours, housing the cutting-edge technology of the city. Here advertising agencies rub shoulders with TV post-production houses and computer specialists. The whole area is serviced and supplied by a plethora of coffee houses, restaurants, bars and the like. Amid the glass and steel of 21st century Manchester sits the John Rylands Library. A glorious Victorian Gothic edifice built of pink Cumbrian sandstone. Dating from the 1890s, it was built by John Rylands widow Enriqueta, who commissioned the architect Basil Champneys to design the building we see today. The library was built to commemorate John's life and houses many of the rare artifacts accumulated by the man himself. John Rylands was one of Manchester's most successful industrialists with an estimated personal fortune of £2.75 million, no mean sum in late Victorian times. The library was one of the first public buildings in Manchester to use electricity and is home to some of the UK's greatest collections of books, manuscripts and archives.

After following the numerous A-Board signs, proclaiming the delights of the Dalton coffee bar and the recently re-vamped library, I pushed on the main door of this wonderful building. I twisted and pulled on the antique knobs: nothing, but a shuddering, wrist-snapping bolted door. So much for marketing. Excuse me, I am not an expert in marketing, but I'd have thought the first pre-requisite of any newly revamped and trumpeted restoration was to make sure the bloody thing was open. Feeling slightly foolish for having well and truly rattled upon the two giant doors, I closed the iron gate behind me and sheepishly rejoined the rest of the bewildered onlookers of Deansgate, along with an equally bemused busload of passengers who had also been privy to my frustrated outburst, whilst waiting at the nearby traffic lights.

Putting the non-delights of the John Rylands Library behind me, I headed instead for one of Manchester's newer attractions,

Urbis. Probably the best explanation of this ultra high-tech, glass-sided building is to be found within their own blurb:

> *Urbis examines, explains and celebrates city life through the experiences and cultures of the people living there. It is about city lives, city voices and city people. With four floors of evolving displays, dedicated to the modern and future city, and an ambitious events programme, Urbis is about covering what's new, original, and interesting about city life, and covering it first.*
>
> *Urbis' programme of changing exhibitions focuses on the culture of the modern city, with explorations of design, architecture, graffiti, photography, music and fashion. The building opened in June 2002 as part of the redevelopment of the area around Exchange Square known as the Millennium Quarter.*

I'm glad they know what it's about, because I haven't got a clue. The exterior is stunning, with its curved front wall and endless mirror panelling. Once inside it reminded me of the Millennium Dome, a celebration building with no set use. The huge open spaces are just that, too open, too undefined, too ill-conceived. The whole thing felt like a very expensive folly. I still love the outside though.

My disappointment was short-lived as I passed under the Palladian façade of the Manchester Art Gallery (MAG). In complete contrast to Urbis, this is a place that knows exactly what it's about. Revamped and extended a decade or so ago, it is bright, impressive and sharp as a tack, whilst losing none of its imposing grandeur. The MAG is home to some of the most beautiful Pre-Raphelite paintings in the UK, and as if to emphasize this point, at the time of my visit it was playing host to an exhibition of Holman Hunt, the Pre-Raphelite master. The exhibits were nothing less than stunning, looking as fresh that day as the day they were painted. Whoever is responsible for the MAG should take the boys and girls from Urbis out for a drink.

Well, I'd done the history, I'd ticked off some of the culture, and seen the view from the Mayor's Parlour, it was time for that other great Mancunian passion, sport. The name Old Trafford is normally identified with football and Manchester United. Less known is the fact that Manchester also has a famous cricket ground bearing the same name, and is but a mere half mile away from its more famous neighbour. Home to Lancashire County Cricket (LCC), it has been the scene of many a test match thriller. Old Trafford is as sedate as the game it represents, a very different place to visit than the home of Manchester United. The LCC has a strong tradition and an even stronger following. For the majority of Mancunians, though, their real passion is reserved for football, and when it comes to this topic you are either red or blue. Rather like dentists and hairdressers, once you've decided which one is for you, there is no going back.

At this point I think I should come clean and declare my status as a life-long 'Red'. Although I have witnessed countless United matches over the years I hadn't actually been behind the scenes at Old Trafford. This oversight was about to be rectified when I joined thirty or so other fans for the 'United Experience.' After coughing up the pound notes (they have to pay these poor players somehow) we were shown the trophy room with its abundance of silverware, before moving into the museum area with its dedicated section to the Munich air disaster. The story of United's first team chopped down in their prime is now fifty years old, but the energy of their youth, the brightness of their ambition and the sheer waste of young life is still evident. From here we were ushered out into the 'Theatre of Dreams', or at least that's what the signboard proclaimed.

"Please don't step on the grass," said our friendly guide.

Bugger. There goes my one chance of scoring in front of the Stretford End. The stadium looks huge when devoid of the loyal fans. It's also eerily quiet. Across an impossibly green, billiard table-smooth turf, the stands rise dramatically through a sea of red seats to the executive boxes, the ultimate prize for the ardent Red. The only noise this morning was that of the groundsman's motor mower as he perfected his stripes across the hallowed turf. Finally we were ushered into the home dressing room. This was where the fiery Scot, Sir Alex Ferguson, allegedly used David Beckham's head for boot-throwing practice. The room itself was very minimal, save for the numbered shirts hanging on their respective pegs above the long benches, everyone instinctively looking towards the No 7 slot. What would you give to witness a half-time pep talk in this room – without ear plugs of course?

In the interests of balanced reporting, or at least a begrudging acceptance of its existence, I crossed the city to Eastlands and the City of Manchester Stadium, the new home of Manchester City Football Club. The boys in pale blue took up residence in this fine stadium some twelve months after Manchester staged the Commonwealth games in 2002. Unlike many host cities who find themselves with an abundance of unused venues when the frantic two weeks are over, Manchester planned its post Commonwealth Games use to perfection. In addition to having a world-class velodrome (the benefits of which were clearly demonstrated in Beijing), the city also gained an Olympic-standard aquatic centre, and several frequently used sites within the sports city area.

By far the biggest recipients from the post-game spoils, though, were the boys in sky blue. One end of this beautiful arena was left open to facilitate the regulation-sized running track for the duration of the games. Once the circus had left town, the guys in hard hats moved back in to complete the final stage of the covered stadium. The result is a masterpiece of modern stadia. Access is via several wide spiral walkways, and the inside playing area, I have to say, is simply stunning. Following three decades in the shadow of their mighty neighbour, and little in the way of silverware to display in the trophy cabinet, Manchester City has, at the stroke of a pen, become the richest club in the world. The new owner, Sheikh Mansour bin Zayed Al Nahyan, is the brother of the ruler of Abu Dhabi, the ruling family of the United Arab Emirates. With an estimated family fortune of $1 trillion (£555 billion) he is set to overshadow Roman Abramovich's Chelsea in terms of financial muscle. The City fans now delight in telling anyone of a red persuasion that the mere act of filling up your car means Manchester City have more to spend on their team. The only bright spot to this unpalatable fact is that as I write, the price of a barrel of crude has dropped below $60. The rivalry between the Manchester fans is, by and large, fairly good-humoured, but I can't end this section without abusing my position and sharing a couple of the more recent Manchester City gags:

A new Man City Oxo cube is to be launched – it will be called a laughing stock.

What's the difference between a lift and a Man City? A lift doesn't take nine months to go down.

I could go on, but that would just be unfair.

The more I delved into the history and hidden places of Manchester, the more I realised I could have written a complete book on the city, rather than a single chapter. No written work on Manchester, however small, would be complete without visiting the scene of probably the most important single incident in this city's chequered history – Peterloo!

On 16th August 1819 at St Peter's Fields in central Manchester, 60,000 people, many carrying banners and slogans, gathered to protest against the punitive Corn Laws and universal suffrage. Rumour, built upon supposition, alarmed the magistrates of the day, and so as a matter of urgency they ordered the arrest of the principal speaker Henry Hunt. At first the Yeomanry were sent in to keep order, but were quickly outnumbered by the protestors. The authorities, now in a panic, over-reacted and sent in the cavalry with sabres drawn. In the mayhem that ensued, eleven people lost their lives and a further six hundred were injured, many seriously. This became known both locally and nationally as the 'Peterloo Massacre.' The heavy-handed actions on this day caused public outrage, but the Tory Government under Lord Liverpool stood firm and instead of showing any compassion or remorse for the tactics employed, passed a new law called the Six Acts, intended to suppress radical newspapers and seditious meetings, thus reducing the chance of an armed uprising or revolt.

A red plaque now adorns the outer wall of what was until recent times the Free Trade Hall, and is believed to be roughly the spot where so many were attacked. Following some lengthy discussion in certain quarters over whether to make the plaque blue or red, red was finally chosen, the consensus of opinion being that 'a red plaque would be more appropriate'. This one is lost on me. What difference does the colour make? If they were campaigning for a life-size statue of a cotton worker slain at the hands of a sabre-rattling Hussar, I could understand the debate. Even an effigy of a lowly worker crushed under an outsized hand of Government, but as to the colour – who cares?

I left Peterloo and the plaque debate and headed for Cathedral Square. Among the many places I have never set foot in whilst in Manchester, the Cathedral must rank as the prime example. If I had a pound for every time I passed it... but set foot inside, no. It's strange, I have visited the cathedrals of Milan, Palma, Paris, Salisbury, Coventry and countless other cities, but for some reason never this one. All that was about to change.

I pushed open the heavy oak door and was met by that all-encompassing cathedral smell. I don't know what it is, but it is unmistakable. Manchester Cathedral is not huge, in fact it feels more church-like, and although quite ancient, it is not at all imposing. Originally it was a collegiate church dating back to 1421, when Thomas De la Warre, the twelfth Baron of Manchester, was granted a licence by Henry V to convert the Parish Church of St Mary into a Collegiate Foundation. It wasn't until 1847 that it became a cathedral.

I entered past the usual 'suggested donation' box (£3) and passed a rather tall verger or similar – it's hard to tell what position they hold, apart from when they are wearing their more obvious ceremonial garb. I mean they don't have nametags like they do in Comet. Having surveyed the usual tombs of past bishops etc, I made my way back to the entrance of the cathedral. There in the open area before the choir stalls sat a stunning black grand piano. A chap in equally glossy black-rimmed specs started casually running up and down the scales. Whether he was part of the church staff or a master from nearby Chethams School of Music wasn't clear. What was clear, however, was that he could certainly tinkle the ivories and had been joined by a pretty young teenage girl who was about to sing.

Her dress code, too, was casual: a pink cropped jacket and faded blue jeans. The casualness of her dress belied her obvious talent. Following a short piano intro, the girl's voice, so clear and haunting, rose into the air, filling every corner of the building and reverberating around the ancient vaulted ceiling. This is how a cathedral should sound. An elderly couple sat nearby absorbing every moment; they obviously knew what was coming. I on the other hand had no idea and was in total awe. I looked once again at the 'suggested donation' box as I left the building and left nothing. Not because I was in a particularly parsimonious mood, more the fact that the experience didn't seem worth the suggested fee. On the other hand, I would have left a tenner if they were collecting for the choir girl.

In a last gasp attempt to gain entry to the John Rylands Library, on a cold and grey January morning, I returned to Deansgate and the previously barred Gothic building. The library is now in the care of The University of Manchester. Only a team of academics could oversee the construction of a stunning £17 million glass and steel extension to the old building and then neglect to place any reasonable signage explaining the position of the new side entrance.

Once through the high-tech reception area, the access stairways continued in glass and steel mode, servicing the major levels of the library. Wow! I did not expect this. Rather like Dr Who's Tardis, the outward appearance defies the complete grandeur of this exceptional structure. Once inside the original building it loses none of the intended appeal, its interior feeing more sanctified than academic. The huge Gothic-style stained glass windows do nothing to dispel this impression. How had I lived so near to this masterpiece and never bothered to visit it? In my defence, if the PR for this building is anything like the experience of the entrance, then I can see why so few people bother to visit.

I chatted to one of the guides who quietly walk the floors of the library on a daily basis (not a job for habitual whistlers or crooners). I had wrongly presumed the origins of the two life-size marble statues that dominate either end of the huge reading room – "Gladstone and Victoria I suppose?"

"Sorry sir, John Rylands and his wife Enriqueta. A common mistake though, sir. The small coronet usually leads people to assume it's Queen Victoria, and the beard John Rylands is sporting, well it's very similar to the one worn by William Gladstone."

I decided at this juncture that the best course of action was to stay silent and let the guide continue with his obvious superior knowledge.

"She was a very determined lady, was Mrs Rylands. She apparently approved the plans for the library in a little over a week, then spent the best part of a decade overseeing every last detail right down to the carved cotton seeds that adorn the back cross rails of the chairs."

As we spoke a young lady approached us and said, "I'm sorry, but I will have to find a quieter place to study," and tootled off in search of solitude.

We both stood slack-jawed, trying to come to terms with this last statement.

"Quieter," I said. "You could hear a mouse stroking its whiskers in here."

"Takes all sorts, sir," he said, sporting a wide smile.

On my way back to the main staircase I stopped to read a carved plaque which read: THIS BUILDING WAS CLEANED DUE TO THE GENEROSITY OF A. CUSSONS.

If this was the soap magnate, it seemed wholly appropriate that some of his vast fortune should have gone to such a clean cause.

Manchester can duly lay claim to many of the major advances brought about by the industrial revolution, and there were few inventions that had a greater impact on society as a whole than the train. Once again this city was at the forefront of train travel. Despite the trials on the Stockton to Darlington line, it is the link between Manchester and Liverpool that really laid the foundation for our modern railway system. Thanks to the foresight of the Manchester Science and Industry Museum (MSIM), it is possible to see and understand just how important that early development was.

The day was turning into one of those so-called 'Manchester days', a leaden sky and a fine rain that seemed to penetrate even the most resilient of fabrics – I just hate this kind of weather, don't you? The MSIM is housed in several of the old Victorian railway warehouses in the Castlefield area of the city. Lovingly restored over the past two decades, they house everything from a hands-on science museum to huge static steam engines and steam locomotives. At the far end of the complex is an underground display, which takes you from Roman Britain through to the present day. Cleverly, the displays and settings encapsulate a sewage system (complete with some rather odious smells), Victorian cellars depicting the appalling living conditions of the early cotton workers, and finally the wonderful Liverpool Road Station complete with its first and second class booking halls. Opened in 1830, it was the terminus for the newly created Liverpool to Manchester railway, and marked the beginning of the Age of Steam. It was to this station that George Stephenson arrived from Rainhill, Liverpool in the famed Rocket, thus establishing the first rail passenger link in the country. Like all things in life, nothing is quite as simple as it first sounds, and the quest to find a working steam engine was no different in this respect. In 1829, as the Liverpool and Manchester Railway was nearing completion, the directors of the company, in their collective wisdom, decided to hold a competition to see if the line would be best served by a static or moving steam engine. Here we have a company that has cut through hills, carved through rock, shifted millions of tons of earth and laid mile upon mile of track, and hasn't got anything to put on it. I can't think of a single modern-day example of such blind faith or complete folly.

The competition took place in October 1829. The locomotives had to pull twenty tons, fifteen times over a distance of 1.75 miles, at a speed of at least ten miles per hour. There were originally ten entrants, but the final contestants numbered just five. By the third day only *Novelty*, *Sans Pareil* and the *Rocket* remained. Well, we all know the outcome, but fewer people are aware that as well as setting a new record for rail travel, another first was entered in the record books.

The opening ceremony for the Liverpool to Manchester line took place on 15th September 1830. Reports of the time talk of a carnival atmosphere at Rainhill; certainly the great and the good were invited to attend. Among the dignitaries who witnessed the historic event was William Huskisson, the MP for Liverpool. Huskisson was riding the line in the same train as the Duke of Wellington. As the train approached Parkside, the train stopped to observe a cavalcade on the adjacent line. Several of the Duke's party stepped down onto the line to take a closer look. Huskisson stepped forward to greet Wellington at precisely the same time as the *Rocket* was approaching on the other track. With the train drawing ever closer, he held on to the open carriage door. Unfortunately, the gap between the two trains was narrowed by the open door. The *Rocket* struck the door, and knocked Huskisson under its wheels. The wounds to Huskisson's leg were described as horrific. He was taken to hospital in Eccles near Manchester, in a train driven by George Stephenson where he died several hours later.

In one eventful afternoon two records were set – the first passenger line in the country was established and, sadly, also the first recorded fatality caused by a passenger train.

I stood on the platform at Liverpool Road Station where George Stephenson had completed his triumphant inter-city journey. Little could he have imagined the huge impact his historic journey was to have.

Outside the Museum, Manchester was living up to its reputation. The rain was still scattering people along the city streets and the clouds were now so low that the last five or six stories of the Bethan Tower – Manchester's much acclaimed forty-seven storey skyscraper – were completely obscured by swirling cloud. The thought of owning the luxurious top floor penthouse lost much of its appeal when viewed on a day like this, added to which, the landmark building is by my reckoning not a million miles from the flight path to Manchester Airport – say no more!

Valleys and Sarsaparilla

Scribe a semi circle on a map directly above Manchester and you have roughly the area of the 19th century cotton trade. From Bolton and Bury in the west, to Rochdale, Oldham and Ashton Under Lyne in the east, in between these major centres sat a myriad of small towns and villages where cotton was the basis of their prosperity. It was said that, at that time, if you stood on any hilltop overlooking Manchester on a clear day, it was almost impossible to count the chimneys. Most of the towns would have been carbon copies of Manchester in make up, but obviously on a smaller scale. The centre of all hope or despair, dependent upon your position in the pecking order, would have been the mill. Spectacularly fashioned at times, these huge structures were in some cases decorated with wonderful Italianate façades and square chimneys, their grandeur standing in stark contrast to the streets of back-to-back terraced houses. These were principally where the cotton workers lived, often in intolerable conditions. In most cases these innumerable terraces were owned by the mill and were very often part and parcel of the job. No job at the mill, no home. There were, of course, always exceptions to the grinding sameness and poor conditions associated with such a huge industry. These exceptions were very often to be found in the more semi-rural communities, where at least you were surrounded by rivers and green fields. The work was no less hard, but what little leisure time there was could be enjoyed in a cleaner environment than your counterparts in the city.

One such area was the Rossendale Valley. The district is made up of four principle towns – Bacup, Haslingden, Rawtenstall, and Whitworth, with a good number of smaller towns and villages such as Edenfield, Waterfoot, Goodshaw, Stacksteads, Helmshore and lastly, sandwiched in between, the delightfully titled Crawshawbooth.

There is something utterly unique in the names of English towns and villages, isn't there? They are so peculiarly representative of our nation that, London apart, no composer has ever managed to write a romantic song about them. If you look to America, you find such classics as *I Left My Heart In San Francisco*, *New York New York*, *24 Hours From Tulsa*, *Chicago*, *Way Down Yonder In New Orleans*, etc, etc. It doesn't quite work when you write *Give My Regards to Crawshawbooth*, does it?

I left the madness that is the M62 motorway. This is a totally personal view, but does anybody apart from Jeremy Clarkson actually enjoy motorways any more? I've long since lost any affection for these giant Scalextric sets, which regularly seem to feature thirty-two ton trucks racing side by side for mile upon mile in the vain hope that one of them may gain a two metre advantage. If they happen to be ascending a steep hill over the Pennines, so much the better.

Once away from the triple-lane insanity of the M62, the M66 link feels like a sedate thoroughfare by comparison, as it gently winds towards the old cross-country route. From here on the surrounding scenery took on a wonderful pastoral calm as I headed into the Rossendale Valley. Although the steep moorland hillsides are still challenging they are softened by agricultural subdivision of fields, pretty farmhouses and darting streams.

I parked up in the near-deserted Rawtenstall (pronounced locally as Rottenstol) central car park. The principal town within 'the Valley', it is also the seat for the Borough of Rossendale. On a cold but clear January morning (and you thought travel writing was all about azure seas and mosquitos), I stepped out into the now hazy sunshine. My quest? The visitor centre.

"I'm sorry love, the visitor centre closed some time ago," said the chirpy lady in the high street baker's. "Try the Town Hall."

Of all the beautiful municipal buildings this area boasts, the Town Hall comes bottom of the list. A monumental 1960s heap of junk, the dispiriting exterior was matched only by the interior and its complete lack of even a single leaflet trumpeting the delights of the Rossendale Valley.

My second port of call was an altogether more pleasant experience. I sidled up to the bar, where the lady of the house drew a half of the refreshing traditional brew. The time was 11 am, a little early, even for me, to be downing a swift half. This time though, I could be forgiven, for the bar in question was Fitzpatrick's, the only functioning Temperance bar in the UK. I chatted to the present owners, Chris and Samantha Law. Chris, who took over the bar in 2000 from the original family owners, the Fitzpatricks, was prior to this venture, a welder.

"It seemed like a good idea at the time," said Chris, "but on reflection, welding was an easy job in comparison to this."

"Not exactly a seamless transition then?" I quipped. He either didn't catch this comment or simply treated it with the contempt it so richly deserved. His wife had joined him in his venture in 2008 and seemed to have plenty of ideas for promoting the historic Fitzpatrick brand. Sam was less convinced though that 'they were in the right area for the retail side of things'.

"If this place was in Manchester, York or London, it would be a different story."

I sipped on my sarsaparilla (how long have I waited to write that phrase?) while Sam and Chris told me the broad history of their Temperance bar. Prior to the Fitzpatrick family opening on this site in 1890, it had been, of all things, a pub called 'The Last Man Standing'. The landlady, a local character gloriously named Zilpa

Duckworth, is reputed to haunt the little bar when the bottles of cream soda and ginger beer have been put away.

The Fitzpatrick family had a chain of temperance bars across Lancashire. As well as the many drinks, such as dandelion and burdoch, ginger beer, blackberry and raisin and of course the renowned sarsaparilla, the bars also stocked a range of herbal teas, potions and sweets. But by the end of the 1930s the game was up, as one by one the bars closed, leaving Rawtenstall as the last of its kind. The wonderful pottery casks, glass bottles and boxes are still on display, but now Chris and Sam have turned their attentions to the world wide web, launching their own site at www.mrfitzpatricks.com. Samantha has resurrected the herbal tea range and is ready to launch them alongside their current drinks products online. I wish them all the luck in the world; they deserve their reward, if only for preserving this little gem.

Whatever shortage of information there had been within the Town Hall was more than compensated for in the many other places of interest within 'the Valley'. The first pamphlet I picked up made rather grim reading though.

> *Records show that by 1830 Ancoats was the black spot of Manchester. The Lancashire cotton industry around this period was employing more than 110,000 poor souls in some 560 mills countywide. Sadly, a third of the workforce were children, some as young as six years of age. Wages for children were about 2s3d (two shillings and three pence) per week (eleven and a half new pence), adults were paid approximately ten times this rate. Hence, it made economic sense to employ as many children and as few adults as possible, and this is exactly what happened.*
>
> *The youngest children were employed to crawl beneath machinery (while still in operation) to gather*

up loose cotton – they were known as 'scavengers' and many died by becoming entangled in the gearing. Many of those who were lucky enough to survive into adulthood had permanent stoops or were crippled from the prolonged crouching that the job entailed. The typical working day was fourteen hours long, but many were much longer, as, free from regulation, unscrupulous mill owners could demand any terms they liked.

This was the grim picture painted by the author of the first pamphlet. Doesn't exactly gel with the Gracie Field's songbook picture of mill life does it?

I was following instructions to the Weavers Cottage and struggling to make progress along the high street because of a fierce wind that was rapidly turning my body posture into a Lowry matchstick man. The pleasant, bright day had turned into a wet soup. I passed the Ivex Mill, a perfect example of a grand stone cotton mill, now converted into rather smart apartments. Whilst on the opposite side of the road sat the very impressive cricket ground, complete with an oval pitch and multi-tiered seating, very grand. I continued along the road until there, in a strangely isolated position, sat the Weavers Cottage. Sod it. Another closed door. What is it with these people? They print brochures, leaflet at random, advertise in papers and list on websites – then, when a weather-beaten traveller like me arrives to view a slice of their precious history, the bloody doors are bolted tight. This example of No Entry was worse than most. Metal plates covered every window, I presume because the contents and the position are somewhat vulnerable, so on this occasion, I couldn't even flat nose the glass to spy on the hidden gems within.

Onward and upward. Rawtenstall today looks as though it has been through some tough times. Firstly, the loss of its cotton industry and in more recent years the demise of its other main income source, the slipper/shoe industry. The latter has in recent years lost out to countless new foreign suppliers from places as diverse as China, Turkey, Poland and Africa. The town is in essence quite pretty, in a rugged sort of way. Many of the stone buildings are grand in stature and even the rising terraces are clean and cared for; they knit into the hillside setting with consummate ease. Sad then, that the same can't be said for the atrocious Asda supermarket that sits like an oversized shed in the centre of the town. I truly do not understand what goes through a town-planning officer's head, if anything, when presented with even an outline sketch of such a monumental mess. Leaving all aesthetics aside, the doughnut effect these monsters have on individual towns and their shopping habits is so well documented that there is no need for one more supermarket to be built – anywhere, ever!

Whitaker Park is approximately a quarter mile from the centre of Rawtenstall and rises from the main Haslingden Road via a pretty winding drive, at the top of which sits Oak Hill House, a huge early Victorian pile. The house was built in 1840 by George Hardman, a local mill owner. It was subsequently purchased by local businessman, Richard Whitaker, who in 1902 generously donated it to the people of Rawtenstall. A wonderfully proportioned house, it commands perfect views over the valley below and, along with many other owners, George Hardman also looked down on his huge mill at the foot of the valley. From the lofty walls of the museum the various pictures of the Hardman family and other local dignitaries look down on you, their eyes following you around the room in that creepy sort of way that quality paintings can appear to. How do they do that?

The house is decorated in convincing Victorian style, and a myriad of artefacts fill the many rooms. Among such items, a stuffed baby elephant seemed the ultimate in one-upmanship for the family who had everything. Were George to return today, I think he would find the whole scene very much as he knew it, the only exception to his view from the upper windows being the tips of two giant wind turbines, part of the new wind farm that tops the ridge over Rossendale. I have mixed feelings on these huge structures. They are, in some strange way, so ugly, that they become beautiful in their own right, rather like someone with pronounced features. I know we are supposed to feel all green and cosy about them, but they are of such monumental proportions that had they not been given their green tag, the first one wouldn't have sneaked past first stage planning. Although looking at the downtown Asda store, I take that back.

Blow me, the sun's come out to play again. How many seasons they get in an average day in these parts is not documented, but variety is certainly the watchword around here. Supposing you wanted to view the largest collection of Tiffany glass on public display outside of New York, where would you start? Paris, London, Venice, perhaps Vienna? Well, you'd be wrong because the answer is Accrington. I repeat, Accrington. The Haworth Art Gallery to be precise. Though technically just outside the Rossendale Valley, I think you will excuse me for wandering slightly off track for this one.

The Haworth Art Gallery sits behind a high wall in an elevated position some two miles outside Accrington, Lancashire. Originally the home of William Haworth and his sister Anne, the children of wealthy mill owner Thomas Haworth (boy these people knew how to pick a good plot), it was originally called Hollins Hill. Built in 1909 in the Arts and Crafts style, it is simply glorious. Sadly, William only enjoyed the house for four years before he died in 1913, leaving the house and its contents to his sister Anne and her companion Miss Priestley. When Anne passed away in 1920 she left the house and grounds, plus a legacy of £20,000 for its upkeep, to the people of Accrington.

If the inside and the contents were anything like the outside, then I was in for a rare treat. The interior lived up to its full promise. The reception hall was grand but welcoming, as was the silver-haired lady sitting behind a low desk.

"We have a very good exhibition of the Haworth bequest including twenty oil paintings and numerous watercolours. Though no doubt, you would prefer to view the Tiffany Glass first? Up the stairs, and all the rooms are dedicated to the various forms and styles of Tiffany glass and mosaics."

I took the wide staircase to the first floor and, sure enough, there in the first room was enough Tiffany Glass to make any collector faint on the spot. This was surreal. Here I was in the heart of Lancashire viewing room upon room of the most splendid glassware outside any private collection. While I viewed the glorious exhibits, I noticed there was also another story that threaded through the museum's display, that of a local man named Joseph Briggs, the person responsible for collecting and eventually giving the collection to the people of Accrington.

In 1891 Joseph Briggs, just seventeen years of age, left his hometown to seek 'fame and fortune' in America. Just how fortuitous this move was to prove, nobody could have predicted. A chance meeting with Louis Comfort Tiffany, the head of the company that bore his name and the primary exponent of Art Noveau glass, led to Joseph joining the company in 1893. He rapidly became a key figure within Tiffany, remaining with them until their closure in 1933. Prior to the closure, Joseph had the foresight to send a shipment of vases, mosaics and tiles (one hundred and forty pieces in all) back to Accrington. The glass went into safe storage for the duration of the Second World War, and it wasn't until 1951 that it found a permanent home at the Haworth gallery.

The sheer volume of original pieces tends to blind the visitor to just how stunning this glass is. One piece would look sensational in a room; one hundred and forty examples is akin to a chocoholic spending an evening inside Cadbury's.

I returned to the ground floor and my friendly attendant, who in my absence had obviously decided that I was a fit candidate for the mouse test.

"Within the main sitting room, hidden in the carved panelling or the fireplace is a small mouse, the trademark of the carver. I will leave you for a couple of moments, see if you can spot where it is."

What else could I do? This was her obvious high spot on a quiet January afternoon – I suppose you could call it a game of cat and mouse, but just who was the cat? I'm not sure, but I had the distinct feeling it wasn't me.

"Have you found him yet?" said my tormentor on her return.

"Sorry, I can't see him anywhere."

The challenge then took on a new twist as we changed to a game of hot and cold.

"You're very warm," she said as I approached the large carved fireplace. "Very warm indeed."

"Ah – I can see him," I exclaimed, joining in the game. "He's right under the top lip of the mantelpiece."

"Very few people spot him straight away. You have to really concentrate, don't you?"

"You do indeed," I replied.

How much fun can you pack into one visit to a gallery?

The pathway to the Top o' Slate (originally the site of an old quarry) was steep and challenging, not helped by the horizontal wind, now creating an extra parting in my hair. This was definitely not the place for anyone wearing a toupee. My destination in this biting wind? The steel sculpture Halo, designed by John Kennedy of Land Lab, one of four panopticons on prominent view across Pennine Lancashire. Their purpose? To proclaim to the world the 'regeneration of East Lancashire'.

Wow, this is some structure. Looking for all the world as though it has landed from outer space during the night, it is certainly challenging to the senses. It could best be described as a huge mesh bowl with serrated arms set on top of a tubular metal tripod. As dusk falls it can be clearly seen from miles away, bathed in a multitude of deep blue lights, reinforcing its extra-terrestrial image. The views from this hill are equally impressive: on one side the snaking ridge of the Pennines, whilst on the other Accrington and Blackburn, once proud cotton towns, spread out to the horizon.

The only other visitor to this windswept edifice was a man of advancing years, who, with sturdy walking stick in hand, nodded and said, "Halo."

"Hello," I replied.

"No. That's its name."

"What?" I replied.

"The flying saucer, it's called Halo."

"Oh I see," I replied, feeling rather stupid.

"They put it up here as a symbol of future, 'ope and prospurity for the area, can't say it's done us much bloody good tho. Apart from the fella's as erected it, there's been no more jobs for the valley as far as I noh."

"Still, it's impressive, if you like modern structures... looks a bit like a spaceship," I replied.

"S'pose so, but the community centre needed doing up before they wittled away the brass on this."

The old boy pulled up his collar and started off down the hill, leaving me with a parting shot.

"If it ad been a space ship mind, those little green fellas would be in Manchester bi now, no bugger would stay in Hasligden unless ee as-to."

Whatever the elements and life in general has thrown at this district and its people over the centuries, it has done little to dent their genuine kindness and warmth of character, the accent only adding to the charm. The people of 'the Valley' have adopted a lovely rounded vowel sound, often with the accent on the first syllable and a rolling of the letter R. Imagine you were listening to Vernon Kay, or the one-time Liberal MP, Cyril Smith. Yes, on reflection you can certainly say that the inhabitants of Rossendale certainly know how to roll their Rs.

Wool and Odd Practices

If Liverpool was the centre of the nineteenth century sea trade, and Manchester was the land of cotton, then Leeds-Bradford was all things woollen. Despite its unfair reputation as the 'rainy capital' of the UK, Manchester and its near neighbours did offer the perfect conditions for spinning cotton, not because it rained more, but because the dampness lingered in the low-lying areas around the city. On the other side of the Pennines, Yorkshire was considered the perfect area for the rapidly expanding woollen trade. Rather like its people, Yorkshire had that essential dryness, and was considered perfect for spinning yarns.

With the pretty mill town of Halifax firmly in my rear view mirror (yes, Halifax is now scrubbed and very presentable), I drove in the direction of Denholme, a straggling collection of Yorkshire woollen mills and quirky stone houses, set some seven miles from Keighley in the beautiful Calderdale Valley. If I needed to remind myself that I was now over the border, and well and truly in Yorkshire, a quick glance at the names on the map did the trick. Take a look at these wonderful examples – Hipperholme, Shelf, Walsden, Rastrick, Cornholme, Myholm and the wonderfully tongue-twisting Mytholmroyd. You can almost hear Mike Parkinson or Geoffrey Boycott flattening out the vowels.

The morning mist rolled eerily over the craggy West Yorkshire moorland as I ascended the winding hill which led to the village of Haworth. If ever a place was responsible for fuelling the literary imagination, this was it. Harsh hills had given way to a small outcrop of bleak Millstone Grit houses, which even in the now brightening February sun still seemed somehow raw and foreboding. My intended destination, that of so many who had travelled this path before me, was the Old Parsonage, the one-time home of Patrick Brontë, Minister of the Parish and proud father of the Brontë family. A natural fascination for most people will always be how one man sired four equally gifted children. That's right, four children. Besides his much acclaimed daughters, he also had an equally talented son, Branwell. Though his talents lay not in literature, but in art.

I parked at the foot of Main Street, a cobbled thoroughfare with a daunting forty-five degree incline, looking more like the prelude to an assault course than a leisurely stroll up to Haworth Village. You may not have been there but if I tell you that this is where one of the original Hovis television commercials was filmed to the strains of the Largo from Dvorak's New World Symphony, you will instantly picture the natural elevation that stretched out before me. At the summit of Main Street (and I use the word summit in its literal sense) I came upon a small pathway which led to the Rectory of St. Michael's Parish Church, better known as the Brontë Parsonage, and one-time home of the Reverend Patrick Brontë, who took up residence there in 1820 with his wife Maria and their six young children.

I queued behind an assortment of what I will kindly describe as people of advancing years who fished around for purses and wallets hidden deep in mysterious bags and hold-alls, patiently waiting whilst they sorted out the necessary coins for entrance to the Brontë Parsonage Museum. The attendant, with super-human tolerance and a genuinely warm smile, greeted each visitor and sent them tottering on their way, whereas I, on the other hand, having tendered the correct money, was now two rooms ahead of the befuddled masses.

The Haworth Parsonage is much smaller than one would imagine and sits in a sheltered spot, separated from the church of St. Michael by a somewhat congested graveyard (it really is very full). The rooms of the house are homely and by no stretch of the imagination pertain to grandeur. I mooched through room upon room of informative pictures and artifacts until I came upon what is now somewhat grandiosely titled Branwell's Studio. The third child, and only son Branwell, was obviously the black sheep of the family, and like all black sheep, far more interesting than his more moderate siblings (see *In Search of John Brown* for a more detailed account of Branwell Brontë). It was easy to imagine the Brontë sisters drawing on the surrounding landscape and local characters for their literary inspiration. Even in this day and age the house has a somewhat oppressive feel to it, despite the obvious attempts to soften the Brontë story. The position of their father within the church and the village meant the children were better cared for than most people within the area, but that very position – a child of the rector – brought with it huge responsibility towards the community. This made Branwell's wayward behaviour all the more disturbing for the rector and his talented daughters. Away from the confines of the rectory, life was obviously tough, and the village of Haworth no exception.

After absorbing the Brontë story, I picked my way through the congested graveyard, exiting via the side gate that leads to the moors over Haworth. The proximity of the rectory to the moorlands is very close indeed, and within a matter of minutes, I was standing on a nearby peak where my view was one of wild land falling dramatically to rugged farms and cottages. It didn't take a huge leap of the imagination to see where the Brontë sisters found the inspiration for their books. With the exception of the odd modern farm building, the valley seemed utterly timeless in appearance. Heathcliffe could have been at my shoulder. In the distance I could also trace the path of the Worth Valley Railway (WVR) – my next stop, so to speak.

The Worth Valley Railway is a real gem. British Railways

closed the original line in 1962, leaving little or no public transport to Keighley and surrounding areas. Due entirely to the efforts of local people and railway enthusiasts, the railway was saved and a preservation society formed. Many years of hard work by volunteers and said enthusiasts were eventually rewarded when in 1968 the rail link re-opened to passenger traffic. The line runs from Oxenhope to Keighley, calling at Haworth, Oakworth, Damens and Ingrow West (I wonder what the origins of that last name are?). As well as being hugely popular with day-trippers, the railway has been used on numerous occasions by TV and film producers as the perfect backdrop for their work, never more successfully than when Lionel Jeffries embarked on his adaptation of Edith Nesbitt's classic story *The Railway Children*. Contrary to popular belief, the station featured in this film was not a fictitious place or name; it was in fact Oakworth Station, the second stop on this delightful line. The custodians of the KWVR persuaded the producers to maintain the true station name, a decision that has served them well in the ensuing years.

From where I stood on the platform, Oakworth Station was every bit as perfect as the film depicts, with its timeless colour scheme, scrubbed paintwork, and nostalgic advertising signs. Here Jenny Agutter had uttered those immortal words 'Daddy, my Daddy', a scene that still reduces grown men to blubbering wrecks, myself included. I know it's soft, and I know what's coming, but still, I and countless others fall for it every time – and why not? As if to reinforce the fact that *The Railway Children* had been filmed at Oakworth, the stationmaster-come-ticket-collector was also responsible for the level crossing gates. Whilst issuing my ticket for Keighley, an ominous bell rang.

"Sorry. I'll have to go. The eleven fifteen is on its way."

With this, in true Perks fashion (the stationmaster in the original film), he hurried down the platform crossing the line to close one gate, then rapidly crossing back to lock the other. Almost as soon as he rejoined the platform, a white plume of smoke arose above the nearby trees, as a pristine, black, steam engine hove into view.

I sat back and enjoyed the very pleasant Worth Valley as it glided seamlessly past my carriage window. First stop Damens (only it didn't stop). Next stop, Ingrow West (still sounds like something that would be best seen by a chiropodist). The scene became less idyllic as we approached the end of the line, Keighley, where huge sandstone woollen-mills lay derelict. In any other part of the country these enormous buildings would have been snapped up and gentrified, loft apartments would have been the order of the day. Here, they hadn't been demolished, but simply stood vacant, an embarrassing reminder of better days.

According to the Keighley and District website, 'the town sits within a mile of the confluence of two rivers, the Aire and the Worth. Approximately seven miles from Skipton and eight from Bradford, it is within easy reach of the Yorkshire Dales National Park'. Here the Worth Valley Railway meets the main Airdale line, whilst to the north the Leeds & Liverpool canal gently skirts the town.

Among the many reasons for visiting this Yorkshire town, their new state-of-the-art bus station seemed the primary cause for celebration, I could sense I was in for a rare treat. The only antidote to such high expectation was the fact that the train for Oakwood left at a quarter to the hour.

Devonshire Street is a wide, handsome and impressive shop-lined Victorian terrace, a mere stroll away from the railway station. This was obviously the one-time premier shopping area. Four and five stories high, the buildings are finished in York Stone, the terrace stretching with the gradient of the street for an impossible length. Built to impress, and it did. An equally impressive symbol of Keighley's changing face are the twin domes of the Mosque, the tops of which can be seen, peeping tantalizingly over the lower level of this thoroughfare, looking for all the world like two giant blue tureens with gold knobs. The gentility of Devonshire Street continues into several other pristine areas at the crest of the hill. Then just when you think, well done for taking care of these fine buildings, you stumble on the Airedale Shopping Centre. Saints preserve us! What a tragic mess. Looking for all the world like a plastic leftover from a conservatory exhibition, it is atrocious on every level. I can feel a rant coming on and if this is the best that town planners (and there's a contradiction in terms) can do, then heaven help us. This dispiriting lump has had the usual effect of blighting worthy shopping streets and in the process, reducing them to discount and secondary retail outlets. Whilst the Muslim population of this town considers their building of such importance that they crown it in deepest blue tile and top it in gold, Keighley's council members are content to erect this heap of crap – shame on you! Wow, I feel better for that.

Impressive as the new bus station is, I decided my quest for detail had not yet reached this level. There was however, one recent piece of construction that did catch my eye. Proving that even in a place as ordinary as Keighley, if you dig deep enough you will find something of interest, which is literally what happened, when developers commenced work on the somewhat neglected Royal Arcade. Built in 1901, it was the quintessential Edwardian arcade, the likes of which could have been found in almost any sizeable town across the UK. Managing to survive two World Wars and the onset of modern shopping centres, it limped on until 1987, when it was considered to be unfit for public use. It remained that way for a further twelve years, holding close its unique secret. When the developers finally moved in, they found to their amazement that hidden in the basement section under tons of rubbish and debris lay an underground shopping street, complete with glass fronted units and old advertising signs. The refurbishment of the upstairs arcade continued whilst slowly but surely, the basement area was cleared to reveal its secrets. Access to this subterranean world is via a wooden staircase found towards the rear of the new arcade.

Too late again, this was becoming a habit. After tracking down the management company for the arcade, I was informed that the subterranean tours they had run for the past five years had been brought to an abrupt end, by – you've guessed it – the Health and Safety Executive. Whether it was a full party booking or a single miserable soul like me, insurance had to be arranged. The arcade manager was apologetic and frustrated in equal measure. I thanked him for his time, and he promised to send me any worthwhile update on the situation. I'm sorry, but I'm getting just a little hacked off with our clip-board-carrying society. I don't want to get political or anything, but there are people in the wider world trying to earn a living in a very tough economic climate.

I sauntered back to the train station and my return journey on the Keighley WVR. The platform was eerily quiet considering the schools were on half term. This temporary peace offered the perfect opportunity to talk to Brian, one of the smart uniformed volunteers. He had helped on the railway on an infrequent basis for some time, but when he was forced to take early retirement at the age of sixty, he seized the opportunity to join this happy band, and become a regular volunteer. Brian waxed lyrical for a good fifteen minutes about his beloved railway; these people are immensely proud of this line, and rightly so. As well as being a living time capsule, this is also a working service line for the people of Worth Valley. They receive no help to speak of, in fact the complete opposite is true on some occasions.

"Take for instance last year," said Brian. "It were the fortieth annivesari of owr oppenin, we planned to bring one o' the bigger trains fo the event. What did Rail Track want to switch the points and a bring a big un down the line to us? I'll tell you, £20,000, that's what."

"How much?" I replied.

Brian smiled, "I know, £20,000 – at least Dick Turpin worr a mask."

I looked to the two station clocks, one displaying real time, the other set for the arrival of the next train. The latter was now showing 12.40.

"Well Brian, I suppose my train won't be long now?"

"Yuv plenty o time yet, she won't be in until 1.45."

"But the clock's showing 12.45.'

"Ay, I know, the little hand sticks a bit', yov got an ower o so yet."

I hit Devonshire Street once again, this time in search of scoff. Finding a pleasant coffee bar, with a frontage that resembled an old bank; but then again, half of the buildings in Keighley look like they were once owned by NatWest.

"What can I get thee?"

"I'll have a coffee and a ham salad on brown," was my reply. Sitting on a high stool watching the passing parade, my thoughts were interrupted.

"Weer owt o bran bread, av got bran tacakes tho."

I collected my thoughts and reminded myself that I was no further than thirty miles into Yorkshire and already facing a language problem. "Teacakes," I replied. "What – with currants?'

"No, wi don't put them in, just plain like'.

My sandwich arrived, as big as a dustbin lid and not a currant in sight. As I tucked into my huge teacake, a man of advancing years entered, dragging his left leg pitifully. I thought no more about this until a guy in his early forties came into the coffee bar; he too had a pronounced limp. Odd, I thought, and carried on demolishing my ham and lettuce. Within ten minutes a man in his late forties, with one leg obviously an inch or so shorter than the other limped up to the counter. None of the three knew or recognized each other, what were the odds on this occurrence? Time to finish my lunch and return to the station, I thought, before I found myself cursed by the 'Keighley Limp'.

I sat in the first carriage behind the engine awaiting the familiar judder that would signal our departure from Keighley. My friend

Brian walked by the carriage window, raised a hand and smiled. The carriage door opened and he poked his head around the seat.

"If yor round this wey next Saturday, we've got a big un, as is going up to Settle, it'll be an early start mind, ope ye can mek it."

Wonderful! I'd spent less than half an hour in this man's company, and already I was an honorary member of the KWVR.

A cloud of steam and a rising plume of grey smoke announced our departure. This time I intended to stay on until the end of the line – Oxenhope station. Further down the line between Oakworth and Myholmes tunnel is the spot where Nesbitt's railway children waved their bright red petticoats and handkerchiefs to avert certain disaster when a landslip filled the line. Just to complete the full circle, the house of the doctor featured in the film was in fact the aforementioned Haworth Parsonage. I have had longer train journeys, and certainly more eventful, but seldom more enjoyable. This little line is a credit to all those far-sighted people, who back in 1962 had the wit and wisdom to not only preserve a piece of history, but re-open a valuable transport link. Unlike the beloved Doctor Beeching, whose sole preoccupation appears to have been the dismantling of this country's rail network.

The road from Oxenhope to Hebden Bridge takes you directly over the moors. A steep climb on snake-like roads is rewarded by panoramic views, or at least it is if you haven't got some nut in an Audi Quattro nudging your arse with alarming consequences. At the first semi-straight piece of tarmac, Batman was a fading silhouette, leaving me to park up and take in the Yorkshire landscape. Blimey it's cold out here, the radio report had said it was uncommonly mild for late February and we could expect approximately ten degrees celsius. My car was showing the outside temperature as four degrees, but I reckoned it was well below that. Time for Hebden Bridge and an infusion of coffee I think.

Following several circuits of the town, I found that elusive parking space and ventured forth into the hotbed of activity that is Hebden Bridge. Okay, that last statement may have been a slight exaggeration, but the place was busy, and the pixie sitting by a toadstool in the main square playing a recorder was certainly holding an appreciative audience. Accompanied on the tambourine by a miniature-sized pixie I presumed to be his daughter, his small case on the ground was growing ever fuller with coins of the realm. Stopping to listen for a few moments, I realised that this was probably the only time I had ever heard anybody play a recorder properly, or at least in tune. I'd always associated this instrument with the earnest endeavors of small children, and the often painful results inflicted on smiling members of the family as they sat through a school concert. At last here was the exception to that mindset; he was good, in fact, very, very good.

Hebden Bridge sits in a steep-sided valley, protected from the harsh moorland terrain. Known as the Pennine Centre, its name is derived from the packhorse bridge over Hebden Water. This river crossing became the focal point for the packhorse routes from Halifax to Heptonstall, Burnley and beyond. The Upper Calder Valley was always known for its textile output, but it was not until the advent of steam power that the population of Hebden Bridge started to really expand. The arrival of the canal and rail systems only served to increase the importance of this area to the textile industry. As the population increased, so too, did the unusual multi-tiered houses and cottages that sit at logic-defying angles on the steep rock faces. The textile industry withered and died, so HB set about re-positioning itself as an ideal centre for touring the Pennines and surrounding areas. It also became a very desirable place to live. The town has a very relaxed feel, and although tourism plays an obvious part in the make-up of many of the shops and services, you still get the impression that a good percentage of the people in the busy streets are going about their daily business almost unaware of interlopers like me.

Behind the tourism and the happy visitors anxious for Aunt

Mary's home-baked cakes, there lies another Hebden Bridge – a place of crystals and natural healing, of psychic spirits and holistic treatments. Many of these practices may have become more widely known and used in recent years, but it appears that Hebden Bridge was at the vanguard of such thought. There were certainly enough health food and practical healing shops to satisfy the local population.

On closer investigation there were also a good number of less obvious amenities, such as crystal healing, gem essences, past life regression, energy field treatment for drug addiction, deep oscillation (not quite sure about that one), quantum touch, craniosacral therapy, and a myriad of things I neither understood nor wanted to. The reasons for such interest and availability seemed less clear; I can only assume that ageing hippies hit this sleepy hollow somewhere around the late Seventies and their influence grew steadily from then on. This last statement bears no fact in support, so is therefore purely my own view. On reflection though, I have to say that if I am ever brought low by some disease which cannot be treated by conventional medicine, my best hope would have to be a month in Hebden Bridge.

Whether the various therapies on offer are used by the locals is not documented, but I have to say that by and large they looked a happy and healthy bunch, almost positively gay. Strike out that last comment, I am sat in a pleasant coffee house, chasing the remnant froth of a cappuccino around my cup and unfurling an article I'd spotted some weeks earlier entitled *The Gay Influence In Hebden*. According to the article, 'there are more people with degrees, and more lesbians per head of population, than anywhere else in the country'. I wasn't at all sure why these two facts could or should be related, but I decided that this statement needed a little more qualification. On closer examination, I found there was indeed a reasonably firm foundation for the article. One café notice board offers same-sex civil partnership ceremonies, while the gay pride rainbow flag is proudly flown outside many gay-run shops and venues. Screenings of lesbian films are openly advertised in local shops, and I love this one, there is even a lesbian bird-watching society and hill-walking group. (I'm sorry, I can't see any difference between a gay or straight twitcher). The area is now starting to attract a larger number of gay men, who a couple of years ago would normally have been drawn to the big cities. I have no view on this situation, and neither it seems did the people of this pretty town, none that were openly displayed on this day at least.

The temperature at this lower level had increased by approximately six degrees if my nose was anything to go by. It had returned to a more normal hue; gone was the glowing beacon, always a far better indicator of the true cold than any weather forecast. The sun had even come out to play, be it ever so fleeting, as every five minutes or so it slipped back behind a grey puffball cloud. Still, it was nice to feel the warm intermittent rays on my back.

Across the road from the town square sits the old packhorse bridge, a constant reminder of the town's origins and a testament to earlier construction methods. I wondered just how many heavy-laden creatures had trodden this route? Looking at some of our modern day structures, I can't see many of them looking as good as this one in three hundred years. There again, who's going to be around to prove me wrong?

You'll never know the effort it takes for a proud Lancastrian to venture into Yorkshire in general and Leeds in particular, but in my quest for truth and a semi-balanced book, that's exactly where I am now heading. With Elland Road Stadium (the home of once glorious Leeds United) on my right hand side, I descended into Leeds centre. I've always found the roads around Leeds utterly confusing, and clearly some things just don't change. After finding myself inadvertently on the road for Skipton, I managed the impossible and found a way back that didn't involve a multiple car pile-up or a reprimand from the boys in blue. Ignoring the inner ring road (I've always found difficulty with this concept), modern day Leeds is clean and scrubbed and out to show off.

In the early 18th century the writer Daniel Defoe said: 'Leeds is a large, wealthy and populous town. It stands on the north bank of the river Aire, or rather on both sides of the river for there is a large suburb or part of the town on the south side of the river'. By the beginning of the nineteenth century, the first census showed the population of Leeds to be 30,000, a reasonably large town for the period. That figure had trebled by 1851 when it reached 101,000. In 1848 the first rail service to Derby opened and by 1858 Leeds considered itself important enough to build a grand Town Hall, followed in very short order by the Corn Exchange. Leeds, like Manchester, had arrived. While Manchester derived the majority of its wealth from cotton, the prosperity of Leeds was founded on wool. Before the turn of the 20th century, Yorkshire's influence in all things woollen began to wane. Unlike Lancashire, where the cotton industry would take another fifty years or so to choke and die, the demise of the woollen industry was swift. The Yorkshire acumen soon became apparent, for while the market in the raw material ebbed away, they spotted a lucrative market in the finished product. Leeds and the surrounding area became a huge centre for tailoring. In 1884 Marks and Spencer opened their first penny arcade. The town took on a grander tone as several impressive shopping arcades were rapidly built, principal amongst which were Thorntons Arcade, followed by Queens Arcade, the Grand Arcade and finally, in 1898, the Victoria Arcade. To add to the general optimistic attitude of the time, in 1893 Leeds became a city. In due course, Leeds also became home to the Burton and Hepworth tailoring groups, ensuring that Montague Burton's vision, 'that one day, ninety percent of the British male population would wear one of his suits on their wedding day', became a reality.

It's a strange fact that once you hear certain voices, they are forever associated with certain periods, places or people. I can't read a Clive James book without his antipodean vowel sounds resonating through my brain. In the same way, it is impossible for me to be in Leeds without the languid delivery of Alan Bennett describing how he would catch the tram for Armley and his 'Mam and Dad'. Those inter-war years so lovingly described by this city's favourite son are little more than a distant memory, a sepia-toned vignette of Bennett's own childhood. Leeds today is a mix of shiny steel offices, restored Victorian arcades, and converted mills that adjoin the Leeds-Liverpool canal system as it snakes and dissects the city. The central areas are now home to the usual mix of coffee bars and smart restaurants that inevitably follow in the wake of such regeneration. The day was sharp but sunny and the sky, although at times foreboding, with a distinct lack of fluffy white cloud held any downpour at bay long enough for me to absorb some of the city's finer points.

In the spirit of 'anything Manchester can do we can do better', Leeds has the biggest Town Hall imaginable. Designed by the architect Cuthbert Broderick (don't you just love these names?) who in 1852, at the age of only twenty-nine entered and won a competition to design the Leeds Town Hall. It was built between 1853-58 and it's a whopper. The building sits proudly at Headrow and dominates the skyline as it rises to 225 feet. The clock tower is an even more impressive structure than the front elevation and was added to the plans part way through construction. As it was a council building I presume getting planning permission for this addition was not a problem. Although many of the original council functions this fine building once provided have been moved to less impressive buildings, the Town Hall still holds a special place in the heart of Leeds folk. The building houses the beautiful Victoria Hall, one of the city's principal orchestral performance venues. In keeping with Yorkshire tradition, it also houses one of the biggest organs in Europe – say no more!

Find your way to Swan Street in the city centre and nestled in an unassuming side street sits one of Leeds' little gems, The Leeds City

Varieties. Founded in 1865 by Charles Thornton, a local landlord of some repute, it was originally known as Thornton's New Music Hall. The name subsequently changed to the White Swan Varieties and then Stansfield's Varieties before becoming the City Palace of Varieties. You may have seen the interior of this delightful theatre without even realising it, for this was the one-time venue for the BBC television programme *The Good Old Days*.

Outside the little theatre is a Blue Plaque, which reads:

> *City Varieties Music Hall*
> *Famous venue of The Good Old Days*
> *First broadcast in 1953*
> *Harry Lauder, Charlie Chaplin and Houdini*
> *performed in this Music Hall built in 1865 for Charles*
> *Thornton on the site of the White Swan coaching inn.*

Well, that was about as far as I could get to viewing this palace of variety, because it is currently undergoing an extensive renovation programme and will not be open until the latter months of 2011. The pictures of the work in progress looked impressive; countless original features have been uncovered and are now being restored to their former glory. So once again the people of Leeds will be able to view the glorious crimson and gold interior of this once proud theatre.

The one thing these large northern cities have in common is their adoption of the French-style zoning or quarters. Manchester has a Northern Quarter or Artists' Quarter and plans for more similarly designated areas. The boys in Yorkshire, and in particular Leeds, are no less keen on adopting this continental concept. In their case the Victoria Quarter or VQ is trumpeted to all who will believe and listen as the Knightsbridge of the North. I have to say, it is a very pleasant place to while away an hour or so, particularly if you have a healthy credit card or fat wallet. For here, under or adjoining the stunning Victorian and Edwardian buildings a plethora of up-market goodies awaits, principal amongst which is Harvey Nichols, where yet again I found another proud Yorkshire boast: 'the best Harvey Nichols outside London' – say no more!

There may have been fashion outlets galore but guess what I was looking for? That's right, Caffé Nero. Laying out a map or two of Leeds and environs, I puzzled on the best way to exit this city. Leeds has without doubt pulled itself up by its bootstraps; the shops are glorious, the canal-side apartments sophisticated and alive, the restaurants impressive and the city is clean as a new pin. But oh, this road system! I can only assume that the person who set out the ring roads – both outer and inner – had a Spirograph as a youngster and forgot to take it out of his briefcase! It was no use; I would have to just get in the car and tough it out. I reckoned about three circuits of the city link would do it. Then by chance or design, I thought I might just be able to catch the road for Wetherby and Harrogate.

Tea and Mrs Christie

At approximately 9.45pm on the 3rd December 1926, Agatha Christie left her home in Sunningdale, Berkshire. She left no note or any single clue as to her intended whereabouts. Her car was found some time later hanging precariously over the edge of a chalk pit. At first it was believed she had crashed her car and simply wandered off. She had in fact travelled to London and boarded a train bound for Harrogate. There, Agatha took a taxi to the Swan Hydro (now called the Old Swan Hotel) and checked in under the name of Theresa Neele - the name of her husband's mistress! A nationwide search was undertaken, and at one stage in excess of a thousand police officers and civilians were involved in the search for the world-famous novelist. The area around her home was extensively searched and for the first time, aeroplanes were used to scour the surrounding countryside.

After ten days Bob Tappin, a local banjo player, recognised the author and alerted the police. Colonel Christie was informed and immediately came to collect his wife. Agatha kept her husband waiting before joining him for dinner, putting her disappearance down to total memory loss caused by the car accident. Many people speculated that the disappearance was either a publicity stunt or just a genuine sign of unhappiness or stress and a desperate cry for help. The exact motive for such drastic action was never truthfully explained and, despite several theories, even today it remains as much of a mystery as one of her convoluted book plots.

Agatha herself rarely talked about the incident, simply putting it down to a bout of temporary amnesia caused by a blow to the head. She did however give one brief account of her behaviour in which she stated: 'For twenty-four hours I wandered in a dream, and then found myself in Harrogate as a well-contented and perfectly happy woman who believed she had just come from South Africa.'

Nothing unusual there then!

In 1571 a local man named William Slingsby stopped to take water from a spring near Knaresborough. He must have been well travelled (no pun intended), as he noticed a distinct similarity between the water from this Yorkshire well and the natural springs he had experienced whilst touring Europe. Roughly within the same decade, a physician named Timothy Bright proffered the notion that these waters had 'great healing powers', due to their high content of sulphur and iron. Now comes the clever part. You have discovered something that smells like rotten eggs and tastes like sucking on a rusty iron bar, and you manage to convince the populace at large that this is what they have been lacking for a long and robust life. I'm impressed.

It was 1631 before yet another medic discovered the next major well. This time it was Dr Michael Stanhope who came across St John's Well and wrote of its 'beneficial salt-free properties'. Both this and the Slingsby, or as it is now known, Teweit Well, are to be found in the Stray area of Harrogate - how that name came into use would probably swallow up a whole chapter in its own right. The best was obviously yet to come, as a sulphur spring near the centre of town took on the mantle of the premier place for 'partaking of the waters', and became known locally as The Stinking Spew. In 1804 the Spew was contained in a grand building befitting the sulphurous spring and the Royal Pump Room had arrived. By the height of its popularity in the mid 19th century, the pump room was serving up to a thousand glasses of sulphur water in a single morning.

The Royal Baths followed in 1897, and soon people were coming from far and wide to experience the benefits of one of the largest hydrotherapy centres in the world. On offer was an impressive array of treatments, from sulphur baths to hot springs and mud poultices, not to mention the aromatic drinking water. The baths and pump room maintained a degree of popularity up until the 1960s, when I presume the cures more associated with Hebden Bridge became the order of the day – less smelly and you could wear a colourful kaftan.

Harrogate today is every bit as sedate and genteel as it was in its heyday as a premier Spa destination or when Agatha paid her brief visit. The splendid cast-iron, glass-canopied, Victorian walkways still feature along the impressively wide streets that roll gently down to the centre of this well-heeled Yorkshire Town. The heady Spa days are long since gone, but the town has reinvented itself as a thriving conference centre. It's not unusual to drive through the centre of Harrogate on a bright day in July and hear the sound of a Dixieland band playing in the grounds of the huge Majestic Hotel as the town plays host to the annual gift show or some similar gathering. These regular events have become the life-blood of the many grand hotels this town still boasts. Amongst them, the aforementioned Old Swan Hotel, looking for all the world as it did in those few hectic days in 1926 when Mrs Christie suffered her temporary bout of amnesia. Unlike Agatha, I didn't believe that I had arrived via South Africa but the winding leafy road from Leeds.

On this bright late spring morning Harrogate was a virtual kaleidoscope of colour, principally due to the flowerbeds on every traffic-island and the countless hanging baskets that adorned every lamp-post for as far as the eye could see. The uplifting effect was made all the more pleasurable by the gentle sun now warming my shoulders. Parking my car with ease on one of Harrogate's serene tree-lined avenues, I ventured forth into this delightful spa town. I'm sorry if all this sounds a little effusive, but it really was one of those too-rare days when there is simply nowhere nicer than England, and on this morning nowhere nicer than Harrogate.

The sign outside the newly renovated pump room and spa read:

Back, Neck & Shoulder Massage
Re-energise and relieve muscular tension with this deep massage. Just relax and de-stress as our therapist applies specially blended aromatic and essential oils to ease the tension from your back, neck and shoulders.
Session cost for 30 minutes – £28.00
Chest or Back Wax
Our therapist will apply a honey warm wax to remove the unwanted hair. Afterwards, a soothing lotion is applied to help the skin recover.
Session cost for 30 minutes – £19.00
All of our other treatments are also suitable for men.

The first part of the treatment sounded sublime, the chest wax, less so. Even if the description had been slightly obfuscated by the term 'honey warm wax', the main ingredient – pain – seemed blindingly omitted to me! In the end I skipped both options, preferring to hang on to my curly follicles.

There are, I was informed by several people, two places that any visitor to this beautiful Yorkshire town must visit. The first is that Harrogate favourite, Bettys Café Tea Rooms. Sitting proudly on one of Harrogate's most prominent corners, and sheltered under the most impressive wrought-iron canopy, is the ultimate in calorific temptation – even the exterior looks edible. To stop and linger outside this establishment is not for the weak-willed or serious weight-watcher, and as I clearly fall into the first category I found myself sat at a window seat, simply watching in contented delight as nifty young ladies in starched white tops with brooch-pinned collars and long, continental-style aprons attended to the happy scoffers.

Bettys is not so much a business as an institution. To trace the origins of this famous landmark company we have to travel to Switzerland, where a confectioner by the name of Frederick Belmont looked out one day on, presumably, an Alpine landscape and decided he would like to open his own business. Despite Switzerland along with Austria and Belgium being the centres of fine confectionery, Frederick believed there was more opportunity in England. He arrived at King's Cross Railway Station in 1918 just as the First World War was drawing to a close. Unable to speak much English, he sought directions for the south-west but instead ended up in Bradford before eventually making his way to Harrogate. Here in July 1919 he opened the first Bettys Tea Room on Cambridge Crescent, later moving to their current site on Parliament Street.

By the early 1920s, Belmont had opened a craft bakery, and with the extra revenue this brought he expanded his tea rooms to include York. The origins of the actual name are less clear – some suggest it was named after the Queen Mother Elizabeth Bowes Lyon. This seems unlikely, as she did not come into major public recognition until she married the Duke of York in 1923. Others suggest that the tearooms were in fact named after Betty Lupton, the daughter of a previous occupant. Who knows? But Bettys, with no apostrophe, it remains. In 1962 Bettys merged with the famous tea company Taylors of Harrogate, a natural partnership that exists to this day.

Sat in the delicious surroundings of this most opulent of tea rooms, you can only imagine what would have happened if Frederick had spoken a little more English.

Full of Yorkshire Tea and passion cake, I set off in search of the Old Swan Hotel, the scene of Mrs Christie's sudden amnesia. An impressive ivy-clad building, it sits comfortably halfway up the main road leading out of Harrogate. The reception/lobby is accessed via a wonderful mahogany revolving door. Once inside, you enter a time warp. The lush polished floors and panelled walls induce a calmness and serenity that seemed not a great distance away from the time of Agatha's stay. I wandered freely around the place and took up residence in a comfortable chair within the main lounge area.

Sitting on a far too comfortable sofa, I pondered on the somewhat unusual circumstances that had brought this famous writer to such a place. How times have changed. I cannot imagine that with our constant quest for news and the prurient nature of some newspapers, that even a C-list celebrity could disappear for twenty-four hours without being hunted down by the baying press pack, much less someone of Agatha Christie's standing to simply vanish off the face of the earth for a fortnight... My thought pattern was interrupted by a charming young lady carrying a tray and a notepad.

"Can I get you anything, sir?"

"Sorry, no. I'm just waiting." What was I waiting for, the ghost of Agatha perhaps?

"Very good sir, just call me if you require anything."

"Thank you"

The other must-do when in Harrogate is apparently to visit the Drum and Monkey. Why? I have no idea, but anyone who stayed in the town for the various exhibitions insisted on a ritual visit. So, the Drum and Monkey it was then.

If Harrogate has a more posh place, then the area around Montpellier Place is it. Although I have to add that everywhere around this fair town seemed reasonably posh to my eyes. The Drum is essentially now a restaurant, the bar less of a feature than when its previous owners had nurtured its much-vaulted reputation. I decided to skip any alcoholic intake, what with driving and all that. Harrogate seemed in fine shape and lived up to its deserved reputation: genteel, calm, assured and a pleasant reminder of how many towns and cities should be.

Stereotyping can be dangerous; apparently the Welsh are sombre, the Scots melancholic and Yorkshire men parsimonious. Utter rubbish by and large but there are exceptions, like one landed gent by the name of William Ingleby, son of Sir John Ingleby of

Ripley Castle. Rather than visit his favourite spot in Alsace Lorraine on a regular basis, he decided to model a complete village on the French example. 'Be blowed spending all that brass and wasting all yon time travlin bi boat and such, I'll have me own bit o' France in Yorkshire.'

And so the village of Ripley was rebuilt, *á la* Frog. Unlike his French counterparts, old William was a little more on the sober side – literally. So worried was he that the three village pubs were having a negative influence on the Sunday congregation figures, he closed all three hostelries. The Landlords swiftly packed their bags and departed, and it was not until 1990 that the village enjoyed another licensed pub. That's some drought!

The newly 'wet' Ripley is a picture-postcard place. On a bright day with the sun pleasantly warming your neck, this Yorkshire village does indeed take on the appearance of a French outpost. The buildings certainly appear to have more of a Gallic charm about them than the sometimes foreboding mills and dark terraces so often found in this county's mill towns. With high-pitched roofs, deep overhangs, and neat Gothic-style fronts, the cottages along the main street could certainly have been dropped in from Alsace. The village is light and airy, and as well as the much-welcome Bears Head pub, it also has a gallery and a wonderful aptly named Ripley Store which on first sight, with its deep green and gold frontage, appears more like a mini Fortnum & Mason, complete with a grocer's bike propped up outside and a period style, liveried delivery van – very smart. Inside was even more impressive, with a myriad of specialist foodstuffs and a sweet selection that could have kept you locked in the store for a month. With fresh vanilla cornet in hand, I wandered off to discover a little more about Sir William's French vision.

As part of Sir William's Franglais plans, he copied one idea in particular from the Alsace model. Instead of a town hall, Ripley would have a magnificent Hôtel de Ville – the only one of its kind in England. It wasn't hard to find said building, for the town hall is one of the even more unusual buildings in a village of rather quirky structures. I didn't quite know what I expected to see, but I don't think it was a Pugin-style, neo-Gothic block that now plays host to snooker tournaments, theatre groups, badminton and more. The property now carries the official address of Ripley Star Club, Hôtel De Ville, The Town Hall, Ripley, Harrogate, North Yorkshire. I hope the mail arrives okay.

That day Ripley was busy. The tourists apparently flock here in their thousands and I wondered whether the majority of the interest was due to the obvious charms of the village, or the faux-French connection? I suppose we will never know. For me, Ripley was pretty and pleasant, but apart from the obvious connection to the folks who live in the dominating castle nearby, I couldn't quite get a handle on its mass appeal.

Up Hill and Down Dale

Once the largest county in England by far, Yorkshire covered approximately one eighth of the country. Made up of three regions, it was known collectively as the Ridings – North, East and West. In 1974, in what any proud Yorkshireman will still tell you was an act of 'complete bloody madness', the county boundaries were redrawn. Barnoldswick and the Forest of Bowland were nicked by Lancashire. This one single act would have been enough to send every Yorkshireman spinning in his grave, but insult was added to injury as Sedburgh was gifted to the new county of Cumbria. Then it got worse as the northerly tip including Bowes and Durham, and the top part of the North Riding, including Redcar, became a part of the new county of Cleveland. 'By eck if it didn't get wuss'. East Riding, including the Wolds was subsumed into yet another new county – Humberside. A much reduced Yorkshire was then divided into three administrative zones: North, West and South Yorkshire. If there was a proud Yorkshireman brave enough to say he approved of the new changes, I couldn't find any record of it.

Somewhere in the middle of this odd jumble of old and new boundaries sits the Yorkshire Dales. A National Park since 1954, it stretches from Skipton in the south, to East Witton in the east, and Beck Foot in the west. I have to state here and now to my eternal shame that, apart from crossing Skipton on the odd occasion, I had never really delved into the Dales, so to speak, so this was totally virgin territory for me. I further admit I hadn't a clue what to expect. Sure, I'd watched *Emmerdale* (well, one episode last year, and I'd seen *All Creatures Great and Small*), I'd also been told on several occasions by my dear wife that 'this area is the hidden gem of England' and furthermore, that 'if everybody suddenly visited the Dales they would want to up sticks and move there, so it was probably better that its charms remain a well guarded secret'.

Looking at the map, I could clearly see there were several ways of reaching the Dales. By far the simplest appeared to be the road from Harrogate to Bubberhouses through Hazlewood with Stonths (what brilliant names) and on to Bolton Abbey.

The word 'dale' is believed to have originated from the Nordic word for valley, hence the suffix to so many of the place names within the area. Although the term appears in other parts of Yorkshire, since the creation of the National Park in 1954, it nearly always refers to the specific area east of the Vale of York. The Dales in most cases take their name from the local river or stream: Airedale, Wharfdale, Calderdale one obvious exception being Wensleydale, and everyone knows that's named after Wallace's favourite cheese, so this seemed as good a place to start as any. Taking random selection to its ultimate conclusion, I looked at the map and noted that Wensleydale is sub-divided into several sections. This was becoming a complete gamble; no planning, no preconceived ideas or information to influence my decision, this was kismet!

Well, where was fate about to take me? I'll tell you – Askrigg, that's where. The destination could so easily have been Simonstone, Thoralby, Gayle or Aysgarth, but there was something about the name Askrigg that simply jumped off the page; it sounded more akin to a Viking warrior than a village in the Dales I knew nothing about the place, and wasn't even 100% sure of how to get there – but hey, let's take a chance, come with me to Askrigg. After consulting my trusty road atlas I realised that Wensleydale was almost in the middle of the Dales, and Askrigg sat in Upper Wensleydale, just about as far into Wensleydale as you could get. All my previous plans were of little use, so instead of travelling southward through the Dales I set my compass to due west.

Surprise, surprise, like thousands of others I'd never actually been to Askrigg before, but I had seen parts of it without even realising it. Askrigg, it turns out, was the fictional village setting of Darrowby in the BBC television series *All Creatures Great and Small*, which was based on a collection of stories by James Herriot. Here in this pretty, rugged Yorkshire village, the irascible Robert Hardy (Siegfried Farnon), the ever-moderate Christopher Timothy (James Herriot), the affable Peter Davison (Tristan Farnon) and the ever-calming Lynda Bellingham (Helen Herriot), filmed the hugely successful four series.

Approached via a winding, tumbling road that seemed to abruptly deposit you in a protected valley the high, craggy hills were now framing a protective wall around this isolated village. Not until I parked up did I realise its exact location, and Askrigg's actual claim to fame. Any doubts that this sleepy village might one day slip back into peaceful obscurity seemed to be based more on hope than reality if the volume of tourists out and about today was anything to go by as it was really rather crowded. In fairness to Askrigg, not all the visitors on this day were Herriot fans. Among the usual white haired trippers there was a good smattering of hill walkers – and I mean serious walkers – you know, rolled maps, stout boots with those peculiar golden laces, chunky backpacks, and despite the warming sun, the obligatory woolly bob hat (I wonder if they keep something special under them?).

Askrigg is everything you would expect from a Dales village, hilly streets lined with lofty stone houses, an assortment of every-day shops, plus the ubiquitous market square and cross. It's worth remembering that this is very much farming country, so like many of these villages, there is also a great deal of local daily activity in evidence. I picked up a small leaflet depicting the various locations used during the filming of *All Creatures Great and Small*. The principal location was the vet's surgery and home, Skeldale House. I followed the instructions for the short distance required and sure enough, there adjoining the local post office was the home of the Herriots. It is a three story, double-fronted, stone house, which is impressive but by no means pertaining to grandeur. It's peculiar how few of these places ever match their perceived setting. Rather like many actors or celebrities (and there's an over-used word), they appear, shall we say, somewhat smaller and less impressive when met face to face. This was exactly how I felt on viewing Skeldale House. I don't know exactly what I expected, but maybe a little more front-age, a garden perhaps, but no, this handsome house was accessed directly from the pavement. Any disappointment I may have person-ally felt obviously didn't transcend to the other Herrioteers in town today. The house seemed to attract a flurry of activity as people of all ages snapped and chatted – one more for the album Ethel! Two ladies of a certain age, and shall we say of generous proportions, pressed me into service:

"Would you mind, love?" as they waved a camera in my direction.

"No, not at all," I replied and set about framing the house as their backdrop. Risking life and limb, may I add, as I stepped out into the road to effect the perfect picture.

"Thanks a lot, love," and my two ladies tootled off in search of fresh photo opportunities.

This event left me with a mental picture of these two gals on returning home, drinking hot chocolate or some similar beverage, and ticking off another TV location:

"Well, Doris, that's *Emmerdale, Heartbeat, Coronation Street, Last of The Summer Wine* and *All Creatures Great and Small* – where to next?"

Other than collecting these locations rather like football cards, I can't see any other reason for wanting to place yourself in front of anything so mundane. The Empire State Building, Sydney Harbour Bridge, or Buckingham Palace yes, but a stone house in Yorkshire? Sorry, it's lost on me. Other than an extended Herriot trail there was, it seemed, very little to hold my interest. So I decided to move on.

I continued in fine fashion across and down the Dales in the direction of Hawes, towards my next intended destination, Settle. The Dales are nothing if not ever-changing. One minute you're driving through serene villages set in tranquil valleys, the next you are crossing open moorland, and then suddenly you are surrounded by rugged crags and glowering peaks. The final miles approaching Settle threw up a completely unique landscape, as giant serrated rock formations closed in upon the road, giving the impression of having suddenly driven into a long quarry. Much of these unusual rock strata can be traced back to glacial passage, and erosion. Over the years since the last ice age, the alternating layers of limestone and millstone grit have left either rolling hills or, as in this case, Yorkshire's own answer to the Grand Canyon.

Settle is ruggedly pretty. Nestling under rising peaks, its streets wind and undulate, and roughly halfway along the main street, accessed via a side road, sits Settle Station. And what a station! Imagine the ultimate, pristine Victorian railway building, brightly painted in cream and burgundy, with every last detail right down to the signboards, benches and milk churns, buffed to perfection – well that's Settle. This is a station with a story though, for the Settle to Carlisle line really shouldn't exist, and how it has continued to keep open is an even greater tale. Drift back with me to the heady days of steam. The competing railway companies are creating ever-more unusual routes, and civic pride is matched only by the naked ambition of these companies.

The line was built by the Midland Railway Company following a dispute with the London and North Western Railway over access rights to Scotland. Facing established opposition from the West and

East coast lines, Midland Railway were anxious to offer a third route to join their existing line at Ingleton. In 1865 they applied to parliament for permission to build the line from Settle to Carlisle. The bill was subsequently passed and work started in 1869–70. The project took six years and an unprecedented amount of engineering skill to complete. The line runs for some *seventy-two* miles, has *fourteen* tunnels and *seventeen* viaducts, the daddy of them all being the one at Ribblehead. Although the line was an instant success, and has continued to hold a special place in the heart of the travelling public, it was always going to be a hard business proposition to justify. Had this project been proffered to the average investment company in today's mercenary world, it's safe to say, that the Settle to Carlisle line would never have happened. Thankfully, this was an age where even hard-nosed businessmen could be romantic in the presence of a grand idea, and so this fatally flawed venture became a reality. Hence the reason why I'm now standing in this delightful station waiting for the Carlisle train.

Sad to say, there was no cloud of smoke or white steam from a black locomotive. No, my journey was to be taken on a bright, chirpy diesel hopper, which I didn't mind as I could still cross the Ribblehead Viaduct. I'd booked a ticket for as far as Garsdale Head; this way I could squeeze in some extra time on the edge of the Dales, before moving across to the east coast.

Wow, this is truly spectacular! I'd read about its construction, and I'd seen footage of powerful black locomotives that appeared suspended in the sky as they crossed this high level viaduct, but sitting on a train – even a flashy little hopper – was something else. Designed by the engineer John Sydney Crossley, it spans a huge 440 yards, its impressive twenty-four arches rising to 104 feet above the moors. More than six thousand men worked on the construction of this line, and a good many of them lost their lives while doing so, the largest loss of life attributable to this viaduct. So high was the death toll that the railway company even paid for an extension onto the local graveyard at Chapel-le-Dale. This was all a little hard to comprehend when looking out over the quiet moorland on a near-perfect day. On a slightly brighter note, and as an added bonus, the viaduct is actually curved, so at one point you can clearly see the viaduct and the route ahead – great!

The Settle to Carlisle line was always going to be contentious. Built as previously stated by over-enthusiastic railway barons, the figures never really stacked up. Race forward to the 1980s and the privatisation of the railways. The last thing any accountant wanted on his books was an under-used railway line with more maintenance cost per mile than any other track in the country. Principal amongst their reasons for the line's closure was the Ribblehead Viaduct as it was deemed unsafe, too much to repair, and too costly to maintain. All very laudable when wearing an accountant's head, but what Railtrack and others didn't expect was the emotional backlash.

This isn't just a railway line; to many people it's a romantic wonder of a bygone age, an age where these grand gestures were applauded and cherished. This was, and still is, a giant train set for a generation of boys who grew up with the sight of steam, and the smell of soot as black monsters raced under their nearest railway bridge. The pressure to keep this unique line grew, until it became obvious even to Railtrack and the Government of the day that they would have to retreat. The viaduct I am pleased to say, has been repaired and the line's popularity continues, so much so that only recently one American tourist group voted the Settle to Carlisle Railway, the second greatest railway journey in the world, pushing the Blue Train and the Orient Express into third and fourth place respectively.

The rest of my short journey was a joy and I would like to thank every protestor who hounded the authorities into submission. Sometimes the heart and not the head has to win. I stood on the platform at Garsdale waiting for the return train to Settle and thought, 'isn't life wonderful?'

Although technically out of the Dales, but once again acting on a pure whim, I was drawn towards the little market town of Kirkby Lonsdale, and I am glad I acted on impulse. This is a gem if you are looking for a place to explore the Dales, the Lakes, or the Trough of Bowland. Unlike so many places within the Dales where walking boots and anoraks are the order of the day, Kirkby Lonsdale has that extra dimension of being a place that is enjoyed by locals and tourists alike. Through its narrow streets I wandered, at every bend another alleyway or courtyard caught my attention, each leading to yet another hidden lane or a loop back to the main street. On the corner of Market Street stood the Snooty Fox, a black and white watering hole, all low beams, polished bar and shiny optics. Ordering a half of lager – yes, I know I'm a philistine, and doubly so in view of the selection of beers on show, but I'm driving and lager is lighter for a midday drink – I took my drink and plonked myself in a too-comfortable chair by a large unlit fireplace.

The pub was cool and somewhat tranquil, despite the other customers. These weren't the usual clock-watching lunchtime drinkers, these were people who were savouring their drinks and switching off – probably for the day, or even longer, being that it was near the weekend. They were also distinct in their dress code. There were no hiking boots and thick socks here, neither was there a rucksack to be seen. At a guess these were well-heeled locals. I do love watching people in these sorts or surroundings. Hidden behind a raft of leaflets and brochures, I am sure I appeared harmless enough, but you and I know I was busy making notes.

One chap in particular was holding court. It doesn't matter where you go or which country you visit, in circumstances such as these you will always find a leader, the man or woman who just has to take the floor. His manner, though not abrasive, was measured and assured.

"Well, despite the downturn and all the gloom on the telly, I'd say this area has held up well, wouldn't you?"

General agreement.

"I mean if it hadn't been for that bloody Robert Peston on the box, I don't think things would have been half as bad."

General agreement.

"And do you know the conceited sod won an award the other week for services to broadcasting? An award, can you believe it, a bloody award? I'd have taken him out and shot him!"

Nodding of heads and more agreement. Then a second man piped up: "If you had any bullets left you could save them for Peter Mandelson.

Laughter all round.

These are classic moments, made all the better when people think that the guy by the fireplace is engrossed in a leaflet extolling the virtues of the Lakes.

Once out in the warm sunshine I headed back down the very impressive high street. You can always tell when you have found retail gold, when there are not one but two cheese shops, a wine merchants, a host of up-market gift shops and several very good looking restaurants. What I needed though, was some local guidance to give me more background and a general feel for the place. I found my salvation in the owner of La Maison, a Lifestyle Emporium (so it said on the card). Ann was a gem.

"What sort of people live here?" I asked, "It all looks very well cared for."

"We get a good mix of tourists and locals, but the area has become very desirable over the past few years. There are a lot of small villages around here and the weekenders have made a big impact."

"Weekenders, you mean tourists?"

"No, people from Manchester, Liverpool and even Birmingham who have bought second homes within the area. This has encouraged a lot of the specialist shops to open, and now the good restaurants are moving in. The attraction is that this town is all independents, there are no multiples, apart from Boots, so we have people from Kendal, Blackpool, Preston and even Leeds who travel to shop here."

I thanked her for her time and was about to leave, when she gave me one more snippet of information.

"If you've got an hour or so to spare make sure you have a look at Ruskin's view, and take the Devil's Steps - go down to the end of the street, turn right through St Mary's, and you'll see it. Take care, bye."

What a lovely lady. Guess where I went next? Following the instructions I'd been given, I found myself in a small square surrounded by cottages with no visible exit. At this moment a lady was returning home and had just placed her key in the door. Sensing my presence she swiftly turned.

"Looking for St Mary's?"

"Yes, Ruskin's View actually."

"Thought so, straight along the alleyway, can't miss it," and with that, and before I could say thank you, she was gone. Blimey, they're psychic around here as well.

I took the path that skirted St Mary's Church and rounded a bend to be met by Ruskin's View – and what a view! Situated in a wide wooded valley below, the River Lune, wide and shallow at this point, gently snakes its way through verdant fields creating a near-perfect perspective point, the background completed by glorious rolling hills. When the artist Joseph Mallord William Turner visited Kirkby Lonsdale in 1822, he was said to be totally captivated by what he saw and set about painting the scene almost at once. Turner, who was known to be a quiet and introspective man, is considered by many to be one of our finest landscape artists, and considered this view to be 'without equal'. John Ruskin, artist, poet and art critic, went even further when he visited the town in 1875 stating:

"I do not know, in all my own country, still less in France or Italy, a place more naturally divine."

I think we can take that as a 'yes' for Kirkby Lonsdale and its views.

As instructed, I took the Devil's Steps that descend from this lookout point to the Lune below. I'm not sure of the origin of the name, but they are certainly hell to walk down, twisting from left to right and up and down; they must have been laid by someone who had been on the piss for a week. At the foot of the steps your choice is clear – left, right or straight into the River Lune. I chose the first option, taking me directly away from the town. From here you get a totally different perspective of the river and surrounding countryside. Despite the busy streets up in the town, I had the whole area to myself, a rare treat on a day like today. As I proceeded towards the Devil's Bridge, the shallow waters were busy with small swooping birds and crane fly. For a good twenty minutes I walked by the side of the Lune, all very beautiful and tranquil, but where was the bridge? Five minutes more and then I give up, I said to myself. Ten minutes later, and still no sign of the illusive bridge, I gave up and headed back to the Devil's Steps.

Still puzzled as to their whereabouts, I wandered over to St Mary's Church and slowly opened the creaky door. Wow! What a corker. In truth the church is an obvious mix of architectural styles, the earliest parts I would guess being as early as the 12th century. There are three impressive Norman arches featuring a unique diamond pattern on the stonework, and on the first pillar was a carving of The Green Man, complete with foliage coming from his mouth. Very nice. On one wall was a memorial plaque in memory of the scientist William Sturgeon, who amongst his many achievements invented the first working electromagnet (what, others had invented ones that didn't work?), the galvanometer, and the first successful electric motor. I like the irony of someone so obviously forward-looking being celebrated in what is essentially a village frozen in aspic (in the nicest way, of course). Everything about this church was a joy, even the tower was unique, housing six bells – rather than the usual three or four – the oldest incidentally dating back to 1633 and not clapped-out yet.

I was about to return to the high street, when in a last ditch attempt to find the Devil's Bridge, I stopped a very well-dressed man, his reading glasses suspended on a neck chain and who was carrying a very small dog. I am always puzzled by people who do this, as I believe the average dog has four appendages, commonly known as legs – why not put them to use? Besides which, it does look somewhat camp. No matter, he was very helpful and explained in a very expressive manner that I had taken the wrong turn.

"Go back down the Devil's Steps, do be careful though they are very tricky, turn right, and the bridge is at the other end of the town."

I thanked him and wished his dog a speedy recovery.

Once more down the dreaded steps, and this time hopefully heading in the right direction, I made for the bridge. Despite the obvious beauty found in the opposite direction, this way was far more enlightening. This really is a town that knows what civic pride is all about. Practically every property had been converted or meticulously renovated, and those that were afforded riverside views, had huge panoramic arched windows, and neat rear gardens or balconies. Ten minutes more of rubber-necking and the elusive bridge appeared before me.

As you would expect, there is a legend attached to this bridge, and it goes something like this. One day a woman who was separated from her cow by the river made a pact with the Devil. He would build a bridge across the river in return for the soul of the first living thing to cross the bridge. The woman threw bread over the bridge and her dog followed, thereby tricking the Devil, who had to be satisfied with the soul of an animal rather than that of a human. Not much of a legend really, is it?

On the other hand, it is a beautiful structure. The three-arched, gritstone bridge, supported on hexagonal plinths, dates from around 1370. The large boulders found around the Bridge area are sometimes referred to as the 'Devil's Change', a reference to the spare stone that was scattered as he created the bridge – look, I don't make these legends up, I merely pass on the information. Whatever the reality of its construction, it has certainly stood the test of time, and sits easily alongside the delightful market town. Speaking of markets, that was exactly where I ended up, returning from the river via Jingling Lane (fantastic), which leads directly into The Market Square. As if planned, there was also a market in full swing this day, not a large affair admittedly, but enough to give the feel of genuine usage. The shops around the square included a traditional sweet shop, with shelf upon shelf of equally traditional sweets and sticky goodies. Just to top it all off, the most ornate, castellated, hexagonal market cross fronts the square – it really is over the top. I wandered back to my car, as impressed by this little town as anywhere I had seen to date. I could so easily have driven right past it, so take a tip and make sure you don't!

Hotel On The Rocks

The A64 from York (once away from the confusing ring road system) was a breeze. The only blot on my otherwise-perfect landscape was the weather – where this lot had blown in from, I had no idea, but it was making driving on unfamiliar roads somewhat difficult. I had been forewarned by my dear wife Carolyn to be ready for a surprise once you pass Whitwell on The Hill. She wouldn't say why, but I presumed it would be a pleasant experience.

Ten minutes later I knew exactly what the surprise feature was. Even on a day like today through the mist and drizzle it was impressive. It was Castle Howard, its huge cupola and wide elevation dominating the landscape for miles around. I doubled back and followed the signs for this stately pile, and what an unusual approach it is. The narrow road to the estate stretched out in arrow-like straightness, but rising and falling with the surrounding landscape until it met a pointed arched lodge, which in turn led to the main entrance of Castle Howard.

This is one strange stately home, almost an optical illusion in fact. Unlike most historic buildings on this scale, where they tend to look quite ordinary from a distance and grow in grandeur as you get ever nearer, Castle Howard is the complete opposite. The huge domed, central section and the wide adjoining wings pertain to greatness, however when you stand in front of the main entrance you quickly realise that this is not a four or five story property, but in fact a simple double story building, sitting above a deep basement area.

The castle was built for the third Earl of Carlisle (1669–1738), Charles Howard. As a member of the famous Kit Cat Club in London, Howard mixed with the great and the good. Among the many wealthy individuals and characters he associated with, one of the most interesting members of this select club was the dramatist John Vanbrugh. Vanbrugh had no architectural training or experience whatsoever, when Charles chose him to design and build this house yet he went on to successfully design and construct both Castle Howard and Blenheim Palace. The majority of the construction was undertaken between 1700 and 1710, but the total build time exceeded one hundred years. The death of Vanbrugh in 1726 and Howard in 1738 meant that neither of the friends saw the completed house and the work continued under the fourth Earl until he too died in 1777. With the completion of the Long Gallery in 1811, Castle Howard was at last complete. Castle Howard's most dramatic feature is its central dome. At the time of its construction, this method had never been employed on a private English dwelling and it was met with a mixture of curiosity and awe. Charles had intended to impress, and I think we can safely say he achieved his ambition.

I duly parted with my entrance fee and stood by the stable block (now a gift shop) and waited for the tractor. The rain was now coming down in sheet form and the only way of reaching the house was via two canopied carriages pulled by a covered tractor. The custodians of this establishment had provided this convenience for such occasions and the addition of the covered canopy was a step in the right direction. However, what they had neglected to spot was that in such an exposed place as North Yorkshire the rain blows horizontally as well – the result being that every seat in both carriages was completely soaked, while the driver was warm and snug in his covered cab – great. I coped in true British style by simply swishing away as much water from the seat as possible and perched on the edge of the seat. The elderly chap in the seat directly behind me wasn't so lucky. His solution to this problem could have mirrored mine to perfection, had it not been for his ogre of a wife, who set about interfering and demeaning his every action:

"Don't be so stupid, just look at your jacket, why didn't you brush the water off? Why didn't you sit towards the edge of the seat like the man in front?"

Don't drag me into this, if you were my wife you'd be under the f… tractor wheels by now. How do people get to this level of abuse? I wouldn't speak to someone I loathed in this tone, never mind a so-called 'loved one'.

The tractor chugged the quarter of a mile or so to the house and deposited us, not at the main entrance, but at a rather unimpressive side door. Along a corridor and up a flight of stairs we were asked to proceed until we arrived in the Grand Hall. I was impressed by the sheer height of the central cupola with its circular balcony, but sadly disappointed by the general condition of the grand entrance. I have to defend the last statement in the context of Castle Howard's recent history. Requisitioned as a girls' school during the Second World War, the house suffered a major fire, hence the poor condition of this central area. On the morning of November 9th 1940 a fire broke out in the south-east corner of the house. Rapidly sweeping in a westerly direction, it engulfed the complete dome of the Great Hall and seriously damaged a further twenty rooms before it was extinguished. Among the lost rooms were the Kit Cat room and the Bullseye rooms (what great names), but equally devastating for Castle Howard, was the loss of their prized collection of Canaletto paintings. The sad fact is, large areas of Castle Howard have remained off-limits for decades, the only restoration to a few select rooms coming via the production company responsible for *Brideshead Revisited*, the television series based on Evelyn Waugh's acclaimed novel of the same name.

Not until the final part of the tour do you return to the original opulent rooms and the feeling of being in a stately home, rather than a dispiriting ruin. I chatted to a very amiable lady, just one of the many well-informed guides who patrol Castle Howard on a daily basis. Her frustration was obvious:

"There is no way that the Castle will ever return to its former glory, the re-building work alone would run into tens of millions, and as for the paintings and furniture, well, you couldn't begin to imagine what cost would be involved. Remember this is still a private estate, and his Lordship doesn't have that sort of money."

"Wouldn't it be better to ignore the renovation of the interior and drop an ultra modern wing within the old façade?" I ventured.

"My sentiments entirely," she replied. "Far better to have a living house than this terrible state of limbo."

In case I am filling you with the notion that this place is beyond the pale, not all of Castle Howard is doom and gloom, and by far the most impressive and imposing area for me was the private chapel – it is simply glorious. Dispel any thoughts that this is a minute add-on of some sort, this is worship on a grand scale. Down the left-hand side of the chapel glorious stained-glass panels are set in unique centrally pivoted frames that sit a small distance away from the exterior windows, enabling their movement, to capitalize on the full glory of the invading sunlight. Set under an impressive vaulted ceiling, the chapel's 'altar' is breathtaking, a riot of gold rails and fixtures set on a raised platform and supported by twelve huge Corinthian-style columns. I would have gladly paid the entrance fee to view this section alone.

I stepped out into the glorious grounds and, because the rain had ceased and the sky looked a little more promising, I eschewed the luxury of the tractor-trailer ride and sauntered back towards the stable block, this time without the verbal bombardment of a certain lady – and I use that term loosely.

* * *

Scarborough proudly boasts that 'it was the first real seaside resort in the country, and that people were taking the waters (a reference to bathing not stealing) as far back as 1650'. How this boast by the local tourist board and others is qualified I have no idea. They can't produce ye ancient photographic or video evidence, and not even a great deal of documentary back up, so I think for the moment we will have to take them at their word.

I am afraid my memories of Scarborough are far more recent and, in stark contrast to past events, very well documented. This is how one major event in the town's history was reported by the *Independent* in 1993:

> *A huge landslip was threatening last night to topple one of Scarborough's most prestigious hotels over the south bay cliffs into the sea.*
>
> *The fall of thousands of tons of rock, sand and soil tore open the side of the Holbeck Hall Hotel leaving parts of the building tottering on the edge of the cliffs. Guests were woken shortly after 7am yesterday when cracks appeared in the hotel gardens. Staff quickly evacuated the 50 people staying in the hotel.*
>
> *Throughout the day huge chunks of earth dropped away 200ft into the sea. The landslip was at one point moving at 10ft an hour*
>
> *The 30-roomed hotel was built in 1880 and stands on high cliffs to the south of Scarborough. It is the North Yorkshire town's only four- star hotel and is built in a mock 15th century style with a baronial hall and minstrels' gallery. In 1932 the property was sold to Tom Laughton, the brother of the actor Charles Laughton who occasionally helped run the business in Scarborough.*
>
> *The landslip began late on Thursday evening but it*

was not thought to be a threat to the hotel. However, shortly after dawn yesterday Peter Swales, who lives locally, saw the slip moving fast towards the hotel while walking his dog. He raised the alarm and the evacuation began.

I love the way that even in an article as unusual as this, the *Independent* managed to shoe-horn the name of a past celebrity into their article – very well done.

You won't, I'm sure, be surprised to know that a huge portion of this fine building did in fact end up on the beach below. I was intending to stay in Scarborough this evening, but decided to step at least a promenade-width back from the sea. I rather like the idea of waking up where I went to sleep, in preference to feeling seawater lapping around the foot of my bed.

The earliest references to Scarborough date back to around 966AD and a Viking by the name of Thorgil, nicknamed Skarthi (meaning Hare-Lip). They settled in an area they called Skarthi's Burgh, or Skarthi's Stronghold. It doesn't take a great deal of working out that over the centuries this became Scarborough – it could have been worse, had some bright spark promoted the original translation. The other claim to fame for this North Yorkshire town was the Scarborough Fair. This six-week trading festival was established during the Middle Ages and attracted merchants from all over Europe, leading in turn to the rapid growth in both the town's size and its commercial base. The fair remained an important part of Scarborough for over five hundred years and gave rise to the popular song *Scarborough Fair*. Around the same time as Scarborough was fading from prominence as an important part of the country's coastal defence system, a saviour for the town's wellbeing (literally) was lying in wait. In 1626 a natural stream of acidic water that ran from one of the cliffs to the south of the town was discovered by Mrs Elizabeth Farrow. The spring water was filtered through the rock of the cliff side picking up magnesium sulphate along the way, giving it a similar property to modern day products such as Liver Salts. What Mrs Farrow had actually stumbled across was a cure for constipation. This in turn gave birth to Scarborough Spa. The town began to attract large numbers of visitors from all over the country – hence Scarborough Spa became Britain's first seaside resort. Case proved for the Scarborough Tourist Board I think.

Having surfed the pictures on the web and read the various blurb on Scarborough's hotels and guest houses, I finally plumped for the Helaina on Blenheim Terrace, run by Jill and Tom Wilson. What a good choice, even if I say so myself. I was greeted by Tom who, without any request on my part, found me a larger room than the one I'd originally booked, and still maintained a fine sea view. Set a road width and a lower promenade away from the restless sea, the Helaina was perfect. You know you are in for a happy stay when the shower is immaculate, the towels white and fluffy, and the bed high and deeply comfortable. In addition, the sleek bedside lamps and television performed on the first touch, and the soaps and shower gels were all bespoke, with expensive looking labels and tops. As an added bonus, from my window I had a clear view of Scarborough Castle – this place will do nicely I thought. I have to admit to my eternal shame, I had no idea Scarborough was so big. In my misguided imagination, I had pictured it to be no more than a steep cliff overlooking a pleasant bay, with a couple of streets of neat houses that led to open countryside. Scarborough is in reality very extensive, with row upon row of very tidy, yellow-brick, Victorian and Edwardian houses that either led to the town centre or one of two handsome bays.

After unpacking what few belongings I had and treating myself to a Fair Trade cup of tea (just one of the beverages to be found on my bedside tray), I ventured out to discover a little more about this pleasant spa town. The wind was still sharp but the sun was making a valiant effort to warm this traveller as I made my way up the steep cliffside path that leads to Scarborough Castle. If you are into arrow slits and ramparts then this is the place for you. Unlike many castles throughout the land where all that's left are a couple of old walls and a dried-up moat, Scarborough Castle is in very reasonable condition and it's not hard to see how at one stage it was of premier importance, not only to Scarborough but as part of a larger coastal defence system.

Built in the reign of King Stephen by William le Gros, Earl of Albemarle and Holderness. The castle is situated on a rocky headland, 330 feet above sea level, and sits squarely between the two distinct north and south bays. Its natural elevation and twelve foot thick walls make it the perfect lookout and defensive stronghold. Unbeknown to any potential attacker the castle even maintained its own unique water supply, set under an arched vault towards the East side of the castle yard. Here a reservoir of water known as Lady's Well could hold up to forty tonnes of water (not sure what that is in gallons), but it would have certainly kept a few people watered during any siege. I think we could safely assume that the odds against deposing any inhabitants of this castle were pretty slim. There again, with little else to distract ye olde worlde soldier, I suppose it passed a few interesting hours in a competitive sort of way.

My view on this brightening day was of two distinct bays, each arcing out to the distant promontories and, in between, the delightful hillside homes and hotels. Sitting just below the castle's outer walls is the parish church of St Mary's, a pretty weather-beaten stone church. The history of this site dates back to the twelfth century, however, my visit today was not to uncover another ecclesiastical secret, but a more recent connection, recent in historical terms that is. On Friday 25th May 1849, Anne Brontë, accompanied by her sister Charlotte and a friend, Ellen Nussey, arrived in Scarborough. Anne was very weak and suffering from the late stages of consumption (tuberculosis to you and me). However, she appeared to rally on reaching her favourite place by the sea. The three of them had booked rooms in Wood's Lodgings – the place where Anne had stayed some five years earlier. The following morning she visited the Indoor Sea-water Baths, and insisted she would prefer to bathe alone. Sadly on her return to the lodging house, she collapsed with exhaustion.

On the Sunday afternoon, Anne was well enough to enthusiastically accompany Charlotte and Ellen along the Spa Bridge, where the three of them "took in the spectacular view of the bay". Once again the whole episode had proved too much for her. It was rapidly apparent to both Anne and her sister that she had little time left, and she spent the rest of the evening sitting at the window of the lodging house looking out over the bay. She lasted barely another day and on 28th May 1849 at 2pm, Anne peacefully passed away.

At her sisters' request, Anne was buried in the churchyard of St Mary's and it was here that I stumbled over numerous flat stones and inscriptions in search of the Brontë Grave. Her resting place is not actually in what you would term 'the churchyard'. At some point in later history the graveyard was effectively split into two distinct sections by the introduction of a narrow roadway. Anne's grave is to be found in this separate area – a simple headstone reads:

> *Here Lie The Remains of*
> *ANNE BRONTË*
> *Daughter Of The*
> *REVd P BRONTË*
> *Incumbent of Haworth Yorkshire*
> *She Died Aged 28*
> *May 28th 1849*

From here I headed off towards South Bay via Paradise – no street, road or avenue, this area was simply called Paradise. The irony of knowing I had just gone from a churchyard direct to Paradise wasn't lost on me. Part way along Paradise on the wall of a very pretty Georgian house is a blue plaque – well, you can't pass them by can you? This one was dedicated to Sir George Cayley, 'the father of aeronautics', born 1773, died 15th December 1857. This caught my attention for two reasons. Firstly, the connection to aeronautics at such an early date and secondly, old George had died on my birthday. I'm sure there are countless others who, over the centuries, have done the same, but seeing this event in raised letters, felt strange and somewhat foreboding.

Sir George Cayley, it turns out, was indeed one of the earliest pioneers of heavier-than-air flight and he is credited with two great aeronautical discoveries. He was the first to identify the four aerodynamic forces of flight to weight, lift, drag, and thrust – and the first inventor to build a successful human-carrying glider. So there we have it, well done George! – I think that deserves a blue plaque, don't you?

From Paradise I walked down streets like Sandgate, just one of many pretty streets that tumble down steep slopes to the old harbour. Here delightful narrow-fronted, four storey terraced houses had been lovingly restored and looked cosy and inviting under the warming sun.

No sooner had I set foot on the South Bay Promenade, than the sky blackened and the heavens opened. Bloody hell, where did that lot come from? I darted from canopied shop front to shop front in search of shelter. In addition to the rain a fearsome wind was now blowing in from the east and chilling me to the marrow – great! The time was 3pm and here was I sat under a canopied shelter below the high headland. In front of me the wrought-iron pillars and decorative arches framed a leaden sky, this weather looked set for the day. Instead of giving in and returning to a warm room and a good book, I decided an umbrella would be my only option. The choice was minimal, and so I shelled out the princely sum of £2.99 for a telescopic masterpiece, or at least it was until the first heavy gust of wind turned it into a water catcher on a stick. For the next couple of hours or so, I danced along Scarborough's sea-front and streets, performing dainty spinning turns in an attempt to reverse the condition of my brolly. Whoosh, and the brolly was saving me from the constant downpour, whoosh, and my brolly was an upturned water catcher, another quick pirouette and I was on my merry way. To any onlooker I'm sure I looked like a character from a Jack Vettriano painting, probably entitled *The Dancing Umbrella Man*.

Some things and places pertain to grandeur, carrying descriptions and epithets that bear little resemblance to their position or stature. 'Enormous', 'gigantic', 'colossal', and the recently popularised 'awesome', are just some of the words used to describe the mundane. So when I tell you that the Grand Hotel is enormous it is a statement of fact. Standing on a high promontory above the South Bay, it dominates all. The sheer scale is truly 'awesome'.

When I had read that the Grand Hotel had been rather an imposing place to stay in its heyday I had been a little sceptical. How wrong can you be? I took the Town Train, as this funicular is lovingly called, and in a few short moments, the blue cabin deposited me at the side of The Grand Hotel.

Completed in 1867, it was one of the largest hotels in Europe, which says a great deal about Scarborough's position at that time. The design of the Grand Hotel is said to mirror the theme of time itself. With its four towers, representing the seasons, its 12 floors the months of the year, the 52 chimneys depicting the weeks in a year and the original 365 bedrooms, the days of the year. The hotel was also built in the shape of a V – symbolising the reign of Queen Victoria. How much of this is myth built up over a period of time or pure coincidence it's hard to say, but it's a convincing tale.

The Grand has had a chequered history and its decline has been long and painful. Although the wonderfully ornate stairways and galleried landings are still hugely impressive, they sit at odds with the general low spirit of the place. In the 1950s it was acquired by Butlins, who subsequently sold it on to the present owners, the

Brittania Hotel Group. The Grand has now gone down the £30 per night route, never really a healthy option, but I suppose a monolith like this has to be filled somehow. Inside the hotel was an assortment of old photographs on one wall that lent some substance to the rumour that during the Second World War, the lower floors of this hotel had acted as a command centre for the RAF. Outside is a plaque celebrating the contribution of the RAF personnel stationed here, but no mention of a more secret use. A second plaque was more profound, as it stated that this is the place where, in 1849, the authoress Anne Brontë died. Yes, it appears that this was the former site of the Woods Lodging House. Now, I too looked out over the impressive bay, taking in a view not unlike that of Miss Brontë all those years previously – life is odd.

I trudged back to the hotel in need of a hot drink, some dry socks and a thicker jumper. How miserable places appear when the rain is slowly dripping down your neck, though after an hour or so spent in a dry and comfortable atmosphere, I felt a little more human. I needed to venture out for something to eat, but the rain delayed my return to the streets. Eventually it abated and, donning dry clothes, I stepped out once more to give Scarborough a second view, grabbing my schizophrenic brolly on the way out. However before I could treat myself to a well-deserved dinner I had one more place to visit – Scarborough Railway Station. It wasn't long before the wind and rain returned once more, turning my brolly inside out, but despite the worsening conditions I have to say I found Scarborough rather charming. One minute you are viewing intriguing Georgian and Victorian streets where houses cluster against steep hillsides, the next you are met by Beau Brummel-style squares, more reminiscent of Hove than anything this far north.

I walked the full length of the main shopping street until I reached Scarborough Station. The railway arrived in Scarborough in 1845 as a branch line of the York and North Midland Railway, which in turn became the North Eastern Railway. This rail link became a crucial part of Scarborough's continuing development as a major seaside resort and spa in the late 19th and early 20th century. This unusual grade one listed building reminded me immediately of somewhere else, and as I stood back and thought about it, it came to me – that huge clock-tower with the impressive dome and the wide frontage with its classical entrance – Castle Howard. The same all-front image had been applied, for if truth be known, the interior of the station was really very unimpressive, a sort of all fur coat and no knickers approach. It did however have the longest platform seat in the world, measuring a staggering 139 metres – that's one hell of a lot of bums on seats!

Across the road stood the Stephen Joseph Theatre. At first sight it reminded me of an Art Deco cinema and the banded fluorescent strip lights, now reflecting in the wet roadway, only served to reinforce this impression. Stephen Joseph (the son of Hermione Gingold, actress and film star, and publisher Michael Joseph), when looking around for a suitable venue to test his ideas of 'theatre in the round', eventually pitched up in Scarborough, in 1955. The only mental connection I could make when Scarborough and theatre were mentioned in the same sentence was Alan Ayckbourn. I was aware that Ayckbourn had been a valiant supporter of this town's theatre, staging many of his play's first nights here in preference to the West End. What I wasn't clear about was the venue: I'd always assumed that it was his theatre. Once again I was found wanting in my knowledge of this northern outpost. Alan had begun working with Stephen as early as 1957, when he joined the company as an actor. After performing at several venues around the town it was decided a more permanent home was needed.

Fate stepped in, when the Odeon Cinema closed its doors in 1988; this was the perfect venue for the S.J. Theatre. By 1990 the trust had acquired the property and after several years of fundraising and extensive refurbishment, which saw the removal of the main auditorium and the installation of a complete theatre in the round, the Stephen Joseph Theatre proudly opened its doors on 30th April 1996. Alan Ayckbourn's links with the theatre company spanned five decades and he remained their artistic director until 2009. Well, now we both know a little more about theatre life in Scarborough.

Battered, rain-soaked, but somehow deludedly happy, I headed back towards the centre of Scarborough in search of food, ensuring that every fifty yards or so I did the obligatory umbrella jig – looking for all the world like a bedraggled Mary Poppins. What I needed was comfort food and there was only one option – Italian. I needed cheery music, dry Italian wine, and a man-size pizza, thick with, cheese, ham and sumptuous herbs. Which is exactly what I found at Tricolos on Newborough (that's the name of the street). The interior had been designed to resemble a Neopolitan street-scene, with sand coloured walls and faux-doors and windows, complimented with jaunty angled street lamps and floral decoration. With a dry upper body and head but soaked legs, I took my place in a quiet corner beneath a street lamp. It's a peculiar unwritten law among restaurants, that whenever billy-no-mates enters your establishment, you are obliged to stick him, or her, in a secluded corner. Never mind that he or she may feel isolated enough by not having company, let's shuffle them off into the darkest recess. I wasn't really too concerned as I had to write up some notes, and from this position I could observe the happy diners. The gods had smiled on me this evening. Within five short minutes I was sipping on a truly delightful chilled white wine (where do restaurants buy these wines from?) and, in what seemed no time at all, the smiling waitress placed a dustbin-lid sized, thin base pizza in front of me. I couldn't have felt happier, not even if I had been wearing dry jeans.

The next morning I drew back the curtains of my room at the Helaina – sunshine! Following yesterday's deluge this was more like it. After a hearty full English breakfast (it's odd isn't it? At home I am content to eat a nominal bowl of cereal or a piece of toast, but the minute I sit down in a hotel dining room it's got to be the full monty), I packed my bags and stopped to chat to Tom, my genial host. Originally from Henley-on-Thames he had settled in Scarborough over a decade ago and he and his wife had bought the Helaina five years ago.

"Where does the name Helaina come from?'" I asked.

"We actually inherited it, along with a huge amount of renovation work. At first we thought of changing the name, then we realised that there were hundreds of Belle Views or Cliffsides already in use, so when it comes to looking for a hotel or guest house on the web there aren't many Helaina's on Google, so Helaina it stayed."

I thanked him for making my stay so pleasant and assured him that I would mention him within the pages of this book – so just in case you didn't catch the name, it's the 'Helaina Hotel' – thank you, Tom.

Dumping my bag in the boot of my car, I set off for a last hike. It was obvious that since the disastrous landslip of 1993 Scarborough Council, or whoever is responsible for this area, had made determined efforts to avoid any repeat adverse publicity. The whole of the North Bay boasted a wide promenade with a new sea wall and, beyond the wall, huge stone sea defences had been slotted into position. The morning was bright and cheery as the surfers paddled out on their boards, to ride whatever swell the bay offered. It wasn't exactly St Ives, or Bondi, but it seemed that Scarborough had added another string to its tourist bow.

I walked the full length of the promenade and followed it round the headland to its natural conclusion, South Bay. Unlike so many seaside towns in the UK, where all their prosperity seemed behind them, Scarborough felt different. All it needed was a few more people like Tom, a celebrity chef, nice restaurants and little inventive publicity and Scarborough could be once more in the ascendancy. I liked it very much.

Vampires at Midnight

The car park at Robin Hood's Bay sits approximately a quarter of a mile from the village, and with the whole area a patchwork of double and single yellow lines, there is little alternative but to accept this alternative and place your coins in the slot. What! £4 for two hours? I thought Robin Hood robbed from the rich to give to the poor. Here at the bay that bears his name they just rob from everybody regardless of wealth. The approach to Robin Hood's Bay is steep. Let me rephrase that: the descent down into the village is *dramatic*. I was surrounded by people who were pausing for breath on the way down. I don't mean to be unkind, but the amount of elderly people who, with the aid of walking sticks, were attempting this folly, convinced me that a good percentage of them might never see the car park again.

The origin of the name Robin Hood's Bay remains a mystery. There is little evidence to suggest that Robin of Sherwood ever visited. There are those, of course, who say Robin Hood never existed, so how can anywhere take his name? Robin Hood was in fact the name of an ancient forest spirit or elf and was in widespread use throughout the middle ages. What is well documented, however, is that by the 18th century, this village and bay was thought to be at the very centre of the smuggling trade for North Yorkshire. Protected by marshland on three sides and set on such a precipitous piece of land, it afforded advance warning of any visit from the customs men. It is believed that all levels of society were involved in this activity, from farmers to fishermen, and doctors to clergy. There are documented reports that state that "due to the narrow, darting alleyways and winding streets with their steep steps, custom officials were in mortal fear of being drenched in boiling water or worse". (What could be worse than boiling water?)

The village today is a million miles away from these nefarious dealings; although judging by the car park charges, I'm not so sure. What a difference a day makes. This time yesterday Scarborough was doing its best to turn me into an amphibian, now the sun was warming my face as I sat outside Picnics, a small eatery, sipping on a cool glass of fresh orange juice and watching the passing parade.

The village is a collection of winding streets and solid block stone houses with uneven, red pantile roofs, and steep steps that lead to yet more of the same. Through the centre of the village a stream runs to the sea below. There are shops of all description, several quaint pubs and, at the point where the village meets the shoreline, on a raised rock base sits the museum. It reminded me very much of a Cornish fishing village, the livelihood of the villagers now obviously more dependent on tourists than fish.

Inside the museum were various artefacts concerned with the sea and the village, among them photographs depicting the village around 1880. Looking at this pretty village today it is easy to forget just how hard life was. The women in the photographs wore dark shawls or headscarves, some were smoking long clay pipes, but generally there seemed little luxury to be had beyond the odd glass of ale. The principal exhibits in the little museum, though, were much older than the photographs; they were ancient fossils found within the bay. Due to the very exposed sea floor at low tide, the area is famed for fossil hunting, with the rock pools and beach area being perfect for school field trips and keen collectors alike. There were twenty or so schoolchildren on the shore this day, their schoolmaster carefully laying out all the conditions of the visit:

"Stay in pairs, don't venture past the first cliff, don't climb the cliffs, if there is any danger alert me straight away, and remember, I would like to go back with the same number of pupils I arrived with," – blimey, even I feel nervous now.

I passed a pleasant hour or so walking the headland and then meandering through the upper levels of the village, stopping to read a metal commemorative plaque – which read: Robin Hood's Bay

In 1881 the brig Visitor ran ashore in Robin Hood's Bay. No local boat could be launched on account of the violence of the storm so the Whitby lifeboat was brought overland past this point – a distance of six miles through snow drifts seven foot deep on a road rising to five hundred feet, with two hundred men clearing the way ahead and with eighteen horses heaving at the tow lines while men worked uphill towards them from the bay. The lifeboat was launched two hours after leaving Whitby and at the second attempt the crew of the visitor were saved.

After that it would be a breeze walking back to the car.

Whitby lies at the edge of the North Yorkshire Moors, at the mouth of the River Esk. The town is split by the river into two distinct areas, east and west, and dominated by the sheer cliffs that sit menacingly above.

It's not, perhaps, surprising then, that this was the seaside town chosen by Bram Stoker in 1890 as the setting for his bestselling novel *Dracula*. For some time Stoker had been working on a novel inspired by Hungarian adventurer Arminius Vambery, having listened with avid interest to his tales of the Eastern European living dead, and their constant need for fresh blood. In Whitby, Stoker had found the perfect setting for his masterpiece. The immense foreboding abbey that overlooks the town and the narrow streets, with their dark, challenging alleyways, all added to the developing plot of his novel.

During his stay in Whitby Stoker stayed for some time at a small inn by the river. Each evening at dusk the local pigeons would sit on the window ledge and tap mindlessly at their reflections in the glass. This action was incorporated into Stoker's work and became the sound of *Dracula* as he tapped with his long nails on Lucy's window, seeking attention (and the odd pint if she could spare it). In addition, the bats to the rear of the inn were incorporated into the creepy setting for what, in our terminology, turned out to be an enormous bestseller.

Approached from the moors, the drive into Whitby was very pleasant. The outskirts had the usual mix of tin-shed, out-of-town warehouses (what happened to planning?), though once past the drive-in outlets, the properties became very presentable Victorian stock, well-maintained and obviously very desirable. I parked a good way out of town – not by intent, purely by lack of choice – and sauntered into town. Once again our Yorkshire brothers had extracted large amounts of cash from me under the guise of 'convenient parking'. I personally think it's their way of getting us back for the War of The Roses.

The sun hadn't just returned to remind us of its presence; it was hot. So everybody north of Birmingham had travelled to Whitby for the day, or so it seemed – it really was very crowded. If you decide a day out to Whitby is for you, make sure you cross the swing-bridge to the old town. Here you will find the majority of the original Whitby cottages and you'll be on the right side of the harbour for the Abbey, which is where I was heading. I reached the end of the main street and headed for the 1,000 steps, or it could have been 199 – it felt like 1,000. Either way, they led to the Abbey, founded in 657 AD by the Anglo Saxon King of Northumbria, Oswy (Oswiu). In 867, the Abbey fell to Viking attack, and was abandoned until 1078, when William de Percy ordered that the Abbey be re-founded. Later it became known as Presteby (habitation of Priests in Old Norse) then Hwytby. From this extraction you can see the present name evolving, but not before it was written as Whiteby, ('white settlement' in Old Norse).

By 1220 Whitby Abbey was believed to be one of the wealthiest monasteries in the country. Its accumulated wealth rapidly evaporated over the next few decades, due in no small part to the ongoing building work. On the 14th December 1539 William Davell, the last abbot of Whitby, gave the Abbey to Henry VIII's commissioners under the Dissolution of the Monasteries Act. A little over three months later, the Abbey buildings and land were leased to Richard Cholmley, known as 'the great black knight of the North', who went on to purchase the property. On inheriting the Abbey his son, Francis Cholmley, oversaw substantial changes to the old abbot's lodging, subsequently naming it Cholmley House. Landscape gardens were created in the 17th century and a new wing was added to the house. Sadly, during a violent storm the roof was lost and the decline was rapid from this time on. The abbey church fared little better. Having its roof stripped of lead and subject to regular removal of stone for local building it was left to the mercy of the elements, which believe me would have been considerable. In 1762 the nave fell and by 1830 the tower had crumbled and fallen, leaving the Abbey shell as it appears today.

That was the potted history told to us by the guide, and he looked as though he knew what he was talking about.

I wandered across the wide grasslands that skirt the Abbey, heading in the direction of the coastguard station. Along the cliff top sits a strong wire fence, with bold notices proclaiming: THIS CLIFF TOP IS VERY DANGEROUS – STEEP DROPS – DO NOT PASS THIS POINT.

You know that feeling you get when you see a sign that says WET PAINT DO NOT TOUCH, and you know that you will have to have a little touch, just to make certain that it's wet? Well that's exactly how I felt on viewing this instruction. I knew instinctively that it would be a steep drop, but I had to make sure. In fairness my reckless streak did not take me as far as crossing the wire, but I did find a section where it was possible to peer over the wire to the rocks below, and oh my God, I believe you, that is a big drop – dramatic and fatal. Feeling somewhat queasy (I'm not good with heights) I slowly withdrew to a safer distance and turned tail, seeking safety in the churchyard of St Mary's.

The church of St Mary's sits outside the abbey walls on the same high promontory. This was a fine, dry, sunny day; what it's like up here when the wind blows in from the east and the temperature drops, I shudder to think. The evidence to support such an observation was apparent in the exposed churchyard. The majority of the gravestones were of the grey stone, arched-top variety and on closer inspection all had one thing in common – they were so weather-beaten that all bar a few of the more hardy stones, had entirely lost their engraving. Where once flowing script and precise italics had declared the solemn passing of a life, now there was nothing but a peculiar swirling stone haze, not a name or date to decipher. This was indeed a place where all men were equal in death!

Equally odd is the parish church of St Mary itself, with its Norman tower and quirky 18th century interior. I have visited cathedrals both at home and abroad, peeked into diminutive chapels and generally viewed a good number of places of worship, but never, I repeat, never, have I come across a more unusual church than St Mary's, Scarborough. Principally the interior is the work of local shipwrights, and it shows. Among the more unusual features of this little church are the box pews – one section stating FOR STRANGERS ONLY.

The unique three story pulpit is made even more bizarre by the addition of built in ear trumpets, fitted to improve the poor hearing of a former rector's wife 'so that she may fully hear my sermons' – no modesty there then. The whole of the interior has a galleried area, and where you sat in this church was dependent upon your status in Whitby society. Toffs at the top, etc. Though nobody touched the extraordinary Cholmley pew; this was built in front of the chancel arch for Whitby's premier family – from here they could see and be seen. The whole place is a delicious fusion of Norman, Elizabethan, Gothic, and Heaven only knows what style. Chaotic, weird, unusual in the extreme - and I love it!

I stepped outside into the bright sunshine, and took another couple of snaps of the Abbey, before heading for the one hundred and ninety nine steps. On a brooding winter's night with a full moon as a backdrop it wasn't hard to see how Bram Stoker had dreamt up his blood-sucking character – but this boy was off for a pint of something more palatable.

Sitting outside one of Whitby's ancient inns, I must confess I didn't notice the name but it was something like the Gay Sailor or Dracula's Den, I tucked into something called a Whitby Stuffer. At least I think that's what she called it – I was finding it increasingly difficult to decipher the dialect the further north I travelled. The accent around this area was neither broad Yorkshire or Geordie, in fact it was leaning more towards Northumbrian, that is apart from the Polish girl who had served my drink. No matter, the sandwich was as thick as a doorstep and crammed with everything from bacon to salad and cheese, and topped with some sort of spice, that even now I couldn't readily identify.

I had chosen this particular pub because it had a side terrace overlooking the bay and, to be honest, it offered a little peace and tranquillity, something of a luxury if the milling crowds along Whitby's narrow streets were anything to go by. Unfurling a street guide, I looked for any reference to Captain James Cook. I knew it would be pointless to try and find the little cottage once occupied by this famous son of Whitby, because it is no longer in Whitby – it's in Australia, in Melbourne to be precise. The kind people of this Yorkshire town gifted it to the people of Melbourne in 1934 to commemorate the city's centenary; it was dismantled stone by stone and rebuilt in a central park within Victoria's capital. I know this because I personally visited this diminutive cottage in Fitzroy Gardens, Melbourne, whilst writing a previous travel book – *Return to Oz*. There was however, the street guide informed me, a very good Captain Cook Museum. Great! I thought, that will do.

The Captain Cook Memorial Museum on Grape Lane is a pretty harbourside cottage, accessed via a narrow passageway off Bridge Street. Once again it was a pay job, and once again a lady of certain years with white candy-floss hair relieved me of my hard-earned cash – all my preconceptions about Yorkshire were coming true – ie they don't half like the sight of a 'bit o'brass'.

James Cook was born in the village of Marton in Yorkshire (today a suburb of Middlesbrough) in 1729. His was a humble background; baptised in the local church of St Cuthbert's, he was one of five children. His father, also James, came from Scottish farming stock. By 1741, following five years of education, he began work for his father who had recently become a farm manager. On the rare time he had off from his farm work he would go climbing at nearby Roseberry Tipping. Even this early in life his taste for adventure was evident. In 1745, at the age of sixteen, Cook moved to the fishing village of Staithes where he took up an apprenticeship in a grocery/haberdashery business. The open sea view from the shop window was thought to have inspired Cook's lifelong love of the sea.

If ever there was a young lad not suited to a life of shop worker and general trade, it had to be the young James Cook. His boss, William Sanderson, was astute enough to spot this, and after eighteen months had elapsed, Sanderson took James to nearby Whitby. There he introduced him to John and Henry Walker, prominent Quakers and local ship owners. Their prime trade was in coal and they transported their wares along the English coast in huge barges or brigs. Their house was the place where I was currently standing – The Captain Cook Memorial Museum. Young James was hired as a merchant navy apprentice to serve in their small fleet. The phrase 'duck to water' comes to mind when you think of Cook from this time on. He was assigned to the collier Freelove and for the next five years or so he served on this and other coasters sailing between the Tyne and London. Almost as soon as his three-year apprentice-ship was completed Cook began to travel further afield, mainly on trading ships in the Baltic Sea. His rise through the merchant ranks was steady, and in 1752 he was promoted to Mate (navigation officer) aboard the brig Friendship.

By 1755 James Cook had been offered his own command, but within a month of this offer – on June 7th to be precise – he had volunteered for the Royal Navy. He knew he would have to start at the bottom in terms of rank but he was convinced his prospects would be far greater with the RN. Britain at this time was re-arming for what was to become the Seven Years' War and, once again, Cook's timing proved to be impeccable. His first posting was HMS Eagle under the command of Hugh Palliser. Joining the ship with the rank of boatswain, he set sail under the white ensign in 1756. James was a keen student and a quick learner. He attended Trinity House, Deptford and within two years of joining the Royal Navy, he had passed his master's examination. He was now qualified to navigate and direct a ship of the King's fleet. As well as his obvious navigational and seafaring talents, Cook had another major string to his bow – cartography. He was, it appeared, a natural at survey-ing and map-writing, talents that were to serve him well in future decades.

Such was the reputation of Cook within the Admiralty that by 1766 the Royal Society chose Cook to travel to the Pacific Ocean, his edict to observe and record the transit of Venus across the Sun. He set sail in 1768 in the HMS Endeavour, rounding Cape Horn and then sailed westward across the Pacific to Tahiti, arriving on 13th April 1769. Among his many notable achievements was the mapping of the complete New Zealand coastline, before sailing due west to his greatest discovery.

"It is capacious, safe and commodious." These were the words of Captain James Cook after anchoring in Botany Bay on 29 April 1770. After several days at anchor, during which time his crew landed vast quantities of fish, Cook was tempted to call it Stingray Harbour after the huge fish swimming regularly near the ship. Instead Botany Bay was given its title by the Endeavour's botanists Joseph Banks and Dr David Solander after they stepped ashore at Kurnell on the southern headland and were so overwhelmed by the sheer volume of plants and animals that they declared it 'a unique botanical experience' – hence the name Botany Bay. And so I'd come full circle to Cook's cottage in Melbourne.

The museum was interesting and it was nice to walk around the building where this great mariner had learnt his craft. The exhibits were first-class and the care taken in explanation by way of displays and historical record gave you a very clear idea of both the sailor and the man.

Whitby appeared to be getting busier by the hour. More than the volume of people, it was the fact that Whitby just reeked of food. If it wasn't fish and chips it was the smell of pasties, as people walked along eating these traditional delicacies. I can feel a rant coming on – when did we as a nation adopt this awful habit of eating on the hoof? We know it's bad for us, we know it looks pretty grim, but still countless people indulge daily in street eating – why?

Apart from the Abbey and Captain Cook, Whitby had one more claim to fame, and it was on open display in many of the quaint shops along the high street – Whitby jet. Known from the Victorian era as the mourning stone, it was popularised by the 'Little Lady in Black' (Queen Victoria) following the death of her beloved Albert. This, in truth, is only part of the story. More than a decade earlier Prince Albert and Queen Victoria had visited the Great Exhibition in 1851 and personally admired many of the fashion items – intricate brooches and necklets made from the lustrous black stone – exhibited by the talented Whitby carvers. Jet is in fact a form of fossilised driftwood created over a period of 120 million years and is believed to originate from the Araucaria tree, known more commonly as Monkey puzzle tree. When the trees became imbedded in a thick layer of sedimentary rock they began to fossilise and turn to jet. Now classed as a semi-precious stone, it changes dramatically when polished. Starting as a rough grey stone, it takes on a deep, rich lustre when polished – hence the term 'jet black'. The use of jet predates even the Romans, who particularly liked this deep opaque stone and used it for many of their decorative pieces and jewellery. In fact its use is believed to date back over 4,000 years. Because of the abundance of this material – principally found between the cliffs of Whitby and Staithes, although it was also mined further inland towards Great Ayton – Whitby became the centre of all things jet. At one period in the 19th century there were in excess of 1,500 people employed in the jet industry.

Well that was about it for Whitby. I liked the setting, it had a charming natural harbour and the Abbey and church were compelling. What I didn't enjoy as much were the huge crowds; it was just too busy for me. I could imagine on a crisp winter's day it would be very pleasant; you may actually be able to appreciate the sea air and the narrow streets, rather than the all-pervading aroma of fish and chips.

Oh well – on we go.

Dancing To A Different Toon

If anyone ever tells you that Britain is overcrowded, that there is no longer any space to breathe, that every square inch of the country seems to be built upon, then take them to the Yorkshire Moors. For mile upon mile I drove and, with the exception of the odd tiny village and farm, there was nothing but brooding moorland and sheep. There really is a lot of open space up here.

It would be nice to say that my drive from Whitby to Middlesbrough was taken at a steady pace with enough time to take in the ever-expanding scenery and think about the day in particular, and life in general. Not so. The A62 is not so much a road as a racetrack, and the biggest boy racers by far were the boys in the white vans. Judging by the way they tore up the tarmac along this winding and undulating road, most parcels around here must be delivered within the hour. No sooner had one manic driver tailgated me (and I wasn't travelling at 40mph), than his clone was ducking in and out like a punch-drunk boxer in his attempt to pass me.

I don't think I have ever been anywhere, either here or abroad, and experienced such a sudden and dramatic change of scenery. One minute I was surrounded by mile upon mile of wild, rolling moorland, the next the whole of Middlesbrough's commercial panorama lay before me: waterside cranes, silos, high metal chimneys and industrial estates. It really was so sudden that I pulled over to check my map, just in case I had somehow taken a wrong turning. There was no error, I was on the right track, and this was to be my vista for the next thirty minutes or so as I followed the ever more confusing road signs. Oh great – now I'm on a high-level by-pass trying to pick up the signs for Durham and Gateshead. I have to say for those of you who don't know, I'm not good with heights. Wimpish I know, but I really do not like high-level bridges, particularly when I have a thirty-two ton truck sat on my bumper. Which, if you'd not already guessed, was exactly what happened next.

Searching for road signs and feeling semi-frozen (ask anyone who doesn't like heights what happens), I sweated my way across the huge road bridge that crosses the Tyne Estuary. After what seemed like an eternity, I was back to semi-rural conditions as I headed for Durham.

For the best part of three miles outside the city, the road into Durham is dotted with signs urging you to 'Park & Ride'. Durham is notorious for congestion and, in an attempt to stop people like me driving into town, they provide huge car parks on the city boundaries and a frequent bus service. I am not dealing in double standards here when I say that under normal circumstances I would have taken up their kind offer, but when you have a luggage grip, a camera and notebook, oh, and a pen, and you are tentatively looking for somewhere to stay, then the bus is of little use. Sat in the traffic jam from hell, I suddenly realised that everything anyone had ever told me about Durham was true.

"Great place, but don't bother trying to drive in."

"Super city, but I'd leave the car in an out-of-towner."

And so on and so forth. After what seemed like an eternity, but in truth was no more than twenty-five minutes, I was safely tucked inside a multi-storey car park, never the nicest of places to be, but on this occasion my surroundings felt nothing less than delightful.

Once set free from the confines of the car, Durham is a very pretty town, sorry, city. The huge cathedral, which sits on a large verdant plot looped by the River Wear, dominates the city. There is no chance of ever losing your bearings for, wherever you are, you only have to look up and there it is, towering, all encompassing and majestic. That was just the outside – inside it is jaw-dropping in its enormity. Viewed on a sunny day like today the stained-glass windows were just simply sublime as they threw wonderful mosaic patterns across the floor. It was uncluttered, and yet that very simplicity somehow added to its appeal.

The Norman roof was supported on ribbed columns that appeared to rise skyward forever, so high was the roof. The whole place had a very relaxed atmosphere and none of the money-making attitude of some places. Built between 1093 and 1133, it is thought to be the best example of Norman (Romanesque) architecture in Europe. At the east end of the cathedral is the Chapel of the Nine Altars. This was built in the 11th century and houses the shrine of St Cuthbert, who is still buried here.

Durham is, as I'm sure you're aware, a university city, and so has that immediate feeling of energy, not so much from the activities of the students that day – most of them were happily sitting or lying back on grassy knolls by the riverside. No, this is more a feeling of latent energy that seems to inhabit great seats of learning, a sort of collective expectation – sorry, I think I've spent too long in a car just lately; I'm probably just glad to be back among pedestrians and smiling people.

Durham is compact as cities go. Situated on a rocky peninsula, it alters the complete course of the River Wear's natural transit, the river effectively forming a complete loop around the hilltop cathedral and the quaint city below. The most obvious point of its position being that everywhere you wander there is either a river view or a bridge across the Wear. Wandering around Durham's quaint, winding cobbled streets, with the view of the castle and cathedral enveloped in lush vegetation, it is easy to see why it was voted the 'Best City in the UK' by the readers of *Condé Nast Traveller* magazine. It really is very easy on the eye.

The shops are no less impressive. Galleries, artisan workshops and the like mix easily with cafés, bars and restaurants, making you wish that you had perhaps considered this place for your education – hey ho!

I decided against unpacking my travel grip in this beautiful city, not because I thought for one moment that Durham would be anything other than a great place to unwind in and rest my head for the evening. It was more the fact that if I was being true to my itinerary I needed a few more miles under my belt before I could truly relax.

There are certain things and places that should carry a warning, or at least some form of recognition – like – 'Over the next hill is the biggest bleedin' statue you are likely to see this side of Rio de Janeiro harbour, it will appear from nowhere on reaching the brow of a fairly mundane hill and will just as quickly disappear from view'.

I'm talking of course about the Angel of the North. There I was, casually zipping along a dual carriageway through Gateshead, very little on my mind aside from my intended destination, Newcastle, when – pow – there it was on a hill to my right. I tell you, I damn near crashed the car. The thing is enormous and very close to the road. Designed by Antony Gormley, it stands 66 feet above Gateshead and the outstretched wings have a massive span of 178 feet, so it's not something that you could lose very easily. Work on the metal sculpture started in 1994 and was completed in February 1998 at a cost of £1 million, most of this borne by the Lottery Fund – so you haven't wasted your quid after all. It wouldn't have been Newcastle if there hadn't been a link to football somewhere, for no sooner had the sculpture been officially unveiled than a group of Newcastle United supporters placed a giant Newcastle United football shirt over it, a tribute to their hero Alan Shearer. The shirt came complete with Shearer's name and famous number nine. The police were soon on the scene to ensure its removal, but for a brief half hour Alan Shearer really was the biggest name in football. I have to say that once you get over the shock of its sudden arrival, the Angel of the North is a complete triumph!

After a somewhat torturous trip and crossing more high-level bridges than I am comfortable with (I wanted to enter the city via the Tyne Bridge, but instead ended up on another elongated road bridge), I pitched up in Newcastle and was only too glad to dump my car in the nearest NCP. I then had time to look around before finding a place for the night. It's always a little unnerving when you've not booked in advance, particularly in a city, but I was confident that I would find somewhere. Rather like Durham with its cathedral, there is one focal point that you can always keep in view when taking in the sights of Newcastle, and that's the Charles Grey Memorial. A huge column that sits at the top of Grey Street and dominates all, built in celebration of this city's most famous son Earl Grey (I quite like his tea occasionally). The gritstone Doric column towers 134 feet above the city and is topped with a square platform and guard rail, on top of which sits a thirteen foot Portland Stone statue of the great man. There was, I noticed, a small door in the base of the column, which apparently leads via 164 steps to the foot of the statue. The view from the top of the column is said to be spectacular. I decided to take their word for it, even if the stairway is open to the public. Created by the sculptor Edward Hodges Baily (of Nelson's Column fame), it was erected in recognition of Grey's unstinting efforts in ensuring the Great Reform Act of 1832 became law. Whatever the background for building this monument, it's certainly neck-strainingly impressive, as is Grey Street, the wide avenue bearing his name that leads gently away from the city towards the River Tyne.

I don't know what I had expected the centre of Newcastle to be like, but I don't think I was quite expecting such grandeur. If Middlesbrough and Sunderland had been at the centre of the shipbuilding and engineering trades and had the scars to prove it, then Newcastle was the pretty boy in this triangle of trade.

From the Grey Memorial I walked the length of Grey Street. This most impressive of streets is lined with stunning Neo-Georgian buildings. Built for the most part by John Dobson and Richard Grainger in the 1830s, among its many impressive buildings is the Theatre Royal. In 2002, this thoroughfare was voted 'Best Street in the UK' by BBC Radio 4 listeners – some accolade, eh? Probably the street's biggest fan, though, was Sir John Betjeman. Following one visit to Newcastle he wrote in the most florid terms of Grey Street's charms: 'As for the curve of Grey Street, I shall never forget seeing it to perfection, traffic-less on a misty Sunday morning. Not even old Regent Street, London, can compare with that descending subtle curve'.

I couldn't agree more, John!

After the junction with Mosley Street it continues as Dean Street, following the route of the Lort Burn (once an open sewer that flowed into the Tyne). I walked along a series of smaller and more winding streets that descended ever more rapidly towards the river, until there in front of me was the great River Tyne, and the even more impressive Tyne Bridge. This is simply a wonderful structure, built by men who drank Irn-Bru and bent metal for fun. Looking for all the world like a smaller version of the Sydney Harbour Bridge, it has that same impression of having been dropped into place, like an outsize piece in a model railway. Its four huge pillars and stretching steel approach road simply dwarf the buildings below. The similarity between this and the Sydney Harbour Bridge is no coincidence as the same company – Dorman Lang – built them both.

The sun was warming as I meandered by the Tyne, but the wind sharp and bracing. I could imagine it would lose some of its appeal when the temperature dips to sub-zero and the snow falls on the familiar river. I called in at the Premier Inn Quayside in search of a bed for the night and appproached the young lady on reception:

"Have you got a single room for one night please?"

"Sorry sir, weer fooly booktup. If ya lyke, a cud coll owr other

Premya Inn in toon?"

"Thank you, that's very kind of you."

"Ney boother, it's all part o me job. Yes they have a room, but I'd mek shoower you get there bfooer six, as they soon fill up."

I thanked her once more, and set off with the song *The Fog on the Tyne's All Mine All Mine* running around in my head. The Tyneside accent has been voted one of the friendliest accents in the country and it's not hard to see why 'the fog on the Tyne's all mine all mine, the fog on the Tyne's all mine'.

Fifteen minutes later I was stood at the 'Premya Inn in toon'. This time Stephen, an equally friendly employee of this group, was relieving me of my cash and handing me a plastic card-key, while I joked about the fact that Lenny Henry might be in my room.

"You could really be in luck," replied Stephen, "you might get the one with Dawn French in."

In that case I suppose I'll have to sleep on the floor. The room was bright and had everything I needed, including the most enormous bed. In fact if Lenny had turned up we could have managed perfectly well without bumping into each other.

A relaxing bath, a cup of tea and a thick jumper were required before I could set off to satisfy a manly appetite. Dining alone is probably the most difficult aspect of travel writing. Where to eat? Passing the usual high street fast foodies – Kentucky Fried Chicken, Pizza Hut and McDonalds – I decided they were just too dispiriting to contemplate. Instead, I once again opted for the stodgy comfort of Italian food, at Luigi's in the Groat Market – a homely restaurant, where I was served a piping hot lasagne by a Chrissy Hind lookalike. Accompanied again by a half-bottle of dry, crisp, white wine, I wrote up my notes – by far the easiest option when everyone around is engrossed in conversation. I was mentally miles away, when the waiter came to collect my plate. All I spotted at first was the most wonderful tattooed arm, as it reached across the table towards my plate. I looked up to see a smiling young man, obviously of far-eastern origin.

"I love your tattoo, what is it – a dragon of some sort?"

"Yes, it's a symbol of good luck."

"How long did it take to complete?" I asked.

"About twelve months."

"Not in one go then?"

"No, every two weeks or so I would go for another two hours under the needle."

"Well, rather you than me, but it's magnificent," and I meant it.

I wandered back towards the Tyne because I wanted to see the river and the 'bridge' by night. The temperature had dropped alarmingly by the time I reached the river and I was certainly glad of the thick jumper.

My efforts were rewarded. The Tyne by night is very striking. Up-river, looking spectacular and illuminated by a series of ribbed lights was the 'Eye', or the Millennium Bridge and beyond that lay the Baltic. The Baltic Flour Mill was built for Joseph Rank Limited beside the River Tyne in Gateshead in 1950 as part of the country's post-war urban regeneration plan. Its title is rather more grand these days; since its refurbishment and opening in 2002 it is now entitled the Baltic Centre for Contemporary Art. To complete the evening picture, across the river sat the Sage, a gigantic, balloon-like, steel and tinted glass performance and conference centre. Designed by Foster & Partners and opened in December 2004, the Sage houses a 1,700 seater auditorium and a smaller 400 seater theatre, plus rehearsal rooms and cost in excess of £70 million to complete. This unusual Norman Foster building has been broadly welcomed, though as is usual with controversial architect, not everybody is a fan of his work. Some have compared it to a Silver Slug and, one detractor, a shiny condom. On a crisp night with the moon as a backdrop it looked pretty spectacular to me and certainly adds something to Newcastle's new waterside image.

Despite being known as a city of seven bridges, like its counterpart in Oz there is only one bridge on the Tyne, and if it looked good in daylight, then under arc and spotlights it looked simply bewitching. A final nightcap in a very nice pub and I hit the sack, a tired but happy bunny.

I was up and out of the hotel just after 7am. It's nice to see a city at this hour. The only other people around were bus drivers, cleaners and delivery men. What, the previous evening, had appeared a deeply dispiriting venue – McDonalds – took on an altogether different appeal with the promise of a strong coffee and an Egg McMuffin. The only disadvantage I could see to this choice of location were the seagulls; I couldn't count the number of these grey and white creatures. I felt as though I had strayed onto the film set of *The Birds* as they swooped in low, squawking and flapping alarmingly. They really are quite large creatures when viewed at close quarters and I have to admit I was quite relieved to be inside, rather than a moving target. Muffined up, I ventured once more outside, relieved to see the gulls had flown off to richer pickings.

The Walker Station, like so many other buildings within Newcastle, is bold and impressive. The main front canopy is supported by four huge arches, while the actual frontage stretches all the way to the railway hotel in one direction and the nearby road junction in the other. Now I know why this station is so long, because unlike so many familiar city stations, where the platforms run away from the main entrance, Newcastle's platforms run parallel to the frontage. So what you see when you arrive at the Walker Station is the side of your train, which creates the odd illusion of a giant exterior with a rather diminutive interior – most odd. The city was coming to life, the traffic now heavier and a steady stream of commuters arriving via the station added an extra spark of urgency to the city. I crossed the road, passing an outsized statue of Cardinal Basil Hulme (it really was big viewed at ground level). My destination? St James' Park, the home of Newcastle United Football Club.

I don't think I have ever been anywhere and found a football stadium that features as such an integral part of the city. Set within easy walking distance of every amenity, it really is part of Newcastle, both physically and spiritually. The closeness of the ground to the city means that, when Newcastle are at home, it is impossible not to be aware of their presence. I could see more clearly the importance of football to these people, for there is no way you could escape the roar from this ground when Newcastle score a goal, which sadly hasn't been that often of late. I understood too the feeling of complete desolation felt by these Geordies as their team was relegated last season. At the time, anybody less connected to this city, myself included, found it hard to comprehend the sight of grown men and children openly weeping as the news of their demise filtered through. Standing outside this handsome stadium, within touching distance of this equally handsome city I think I understood a little more clearly the passion and the dented pride.

Back at the Premier Inn, I packed my kit and clobber and left them in the boot of my car, for there was one more place to visit before I departed this fine city. My hotel sat on the edge of a pleasant square that was home to the Laing Art Gallery. As the city clock struck ten, I entered this ultra-modern glass tower. The window posters proudly announced that they were hosting an exhibition of 'Newcastle Reinvented', a collection of watercolours and drawings spanning some two hundred years. Here were contemporary pictures of Grey Street under construction, as well as miners at the pit and ship yard workers on the Tyne. There was no way that football was going to be left out, as St James' Park and the 'common man' were celebrated in a misty work by Byron Dawson.

Among the more permanent exhibits was a painting entitled *Isabella and the Pot of Basil* by William Holman Hunt. You may have gathered by now that I have a particular weakness for Pre-Raphelite paintings, and this one was just as wistful as the others viewed so far. The whole gallery was a delight, and the coffee bar just the ticket, before I said my goodbyes to Newcastle.

I liked this city; the main streets were wide and impressive the buildings cared for and prestigious, and the people cheery and friendly. All in all, my stay had been a more than pleasant experience. I couldn't speak for its more industrialised neighbours like Sunderland and Middlesbrough, but Newcastle was an unexpected delight.

Holy Island

Relieved that my exit from Newcastle didn't involve any more high-level bridges or motorways in the sky, I headed for the A1 and Morpeth. The drive to the county town of Northumberland was pleasant and uneventful, that is if you dismiss the odd lunatic in a thirty-two ton truck or a white van. I hate stereotyping, but sometimes you do wonder what goes through the mind of some of these people – very little, I suspect. Morpeth lies about sixteen miles to the north-west of Newcastle, and is in terms of size and atmosphere about as far as you can get from the Tyne.

Situated within the bend of the River Wansbeck, Morpeth was once a principal stop on the London to Edinburgh coaching route. The origins of its name are thought to derive from the time when it was an access route across the moors – a 'moor path'. Other more sinister explanations point to murder path – its close proximity to the Scottish border and the constant feuding that regularly occurred there would not have been bloodless – take your pick.

Morpeth is a relatively small place for a county town, having a population of barely 15,000. This is perhaps not so surprising, as Northumberland is the most sparsely populated county in England. Though it's fair to say, I think at least a third of those people were out and about in Morpeth that day. After several laps of the area, I eventually found a precious parking space and went off in search of much-needed food.

Unlike Newcastle, Morpeth was never a walled town but it did have a castle. Sadly all that remains is the mound at the Ha' Hill overlooking the town's park. The town is compact and because of its close proximity to the river, has an easy and relaxed feel to it. Although I doubt that this was the case a year or so ago, when great tracts of the town were waist-high in water. This was how the *Guardian* reported the incident in early September 2008:

> *The repair bill from the weekend's flooding is likely to run into tens of millions of pounds, insurers warned today, as forecasters predicted more rain later this week. Storms drenched parts of north-east England, Herefordshire, Yorkshire, Shropshire and Worcestershire. Six people were killed. Worst affected the town of Morpeth, in Northumberland, where four-hundred residents were evacuated and 1,000 properties damaged by floodwater. The environment minister John Healey met residents and emergency services staff in the town this morning. He announced emergency funding for the councils worst affected by the floods.*

Morpeth today shows few obvious outer signs of such huge damage, though I'm sure there are still individuals battling to return to some form of normality. Certainly the people I met on this sunny day were warm and friendly, even if I couldn't quite understand everything they said (the accent this far north takes a practised ear to fully comprehend). My visit to Morpeth was brief, but not so short that I wasn't intrigued by the buildings along the high street. Let me rephrase that: I was intrigued by their height, particularly on one side. Normally the average town house or similar is a respectable two or three stories high. Not so Morpeth. Here for a good distance the properties rose to five stories, and looked most peculiar when the street was viewed in perspective. This was the sort of grandeur usually reserved for Edinburgh or Bath – just struck me as unusual, that's all !

I did however, have one specific purpose in stopping off at Morpeth – apart from food that is – and that was to visit the church of St Mary's, for within this pretty churchyard is the grave of Emily Wilding Davison (born 1872). This may not mean much to you, but if I told you that Emily was probably the most famous Suffragette after Emmeline Pankhurst, her story may strike a chord. In one moment of sheer bloody-mindedness, she would be forever remembered as the woman who lost her life by running in front of King George V's horse, Anmer, at Epsom Derby in June of 1913. Trampled underfoot as the Royal Family watched in horror, she suffered a fracture of the skull. Emily never regained consciousness and she died four days later in hospital. Whether she actually intended to kill herself is something that will always be open to some conjecture. There are those who believe she naïvely thought the horse would stop, and that she would be able to drape the Women's Social and Political Union ribbon around the animal's head. Sadly, if this was her intention, the resulting mayhem was catastrophic. Originally from the nearby village of Longhorsley, Emily was brought home to Morpeth where huge crowds lined the route of her funeral procession before she was finally laid to rest in the churchyard of St Mary's.

Among the many tributes paid to this brave – or some would say foolish – lady, none was more profound than Emmeline Pankhurst's. She described Emily Davison's death in her autobiography *My Own Story*, as follows:

> *Emily Davison clung to her conviction that one great tragedy, the deliberate throwing into the breach of a human life, would put an end to the intolerable torture of women. And so she threw herself at the King's horse, in full view of the King and Queen and a great multitude of their Majesties' subjects.*

In a quiet spot within the sloping churchyard of St Mary's, lies the grave of Emily Wilding Davison. Her headstone bears the simple suffrage slogan: *Deeds Not Words*.

This place had brought me full circle to the drawing room of Emmeline Pankhurst in Manchester all those months previously. Once again I wondered where our modern-day Emmelines and Emilys had gone to? Maybe today's issues just don't call for this level of fortitude and self-sacrifice.

If you were looking for the first place in the world to use hydro-electric power, where would you start? London, New York, Paris, Stockholm perhaps? Well, you would be wrong. For the place you need to come to is Rothbury in Northumberland and the house you would need to visit is Cragside. Built in 1863 for the inventor and industrialist Lord Armstrong (Vickers Armstrong), it was originally a small country lodge but was extended over the following few years. In 1868 a water-powered engine was installed to power all the modern labour-saving devices, such as the laundry and lift. Water was drawn from one of the estate's lakes to power the Siemens dynamo and soon the arc lamps were replaced by incandescent fixtures, in effect the first full installation of electric lighting.

Here we go again – £12 admission – I must have shares in the National Trust by now. I noticed a rather interesting fact as I searched deep within my pockets for the money: I was paying £12 for the privilege of eye-balling Cragside, but a family ticket was only £18. That does it – the next National Trust site I visit, I'm going to adopt three other visitors in the car park. That way we will all get in for £4.50 each!

Cragside, if you've not already guessed it, is now the property of the National Trust, and after that admission charge I think I may own a couple of the roof tiles. Lord Armstrong and his wife Margaret, commissioned R Norman Shaw to carry out the major extensions to Cragside, turning it from the weekend lodge it started life as, into this huge Victorian pile. Shaw, later known for some of the finest houses in Chelsea, was at this time relatively unknown and was teased in later years by fellow architects who said that – 'he must have designed this house in one day while his client was out shooting'. In fairness to Shaw, it is widely believed that Lord Armstrong kept a very close eye on every detail of the house, therefore allowing Shaw very little opportunity to express the talent he so obviously possessed. It has been described by some as 'the most imposing Victorian mansion in the North; others feel it is a monument of folly. Whatever the aesthetics of the building, there is little dispute that it was way ahead of its time in technological terms. Cragside boasted electric light, central heating, and a host of other gadgets including a basement suite of bathrooms that housed a hot air bath, a plunge bath and a shower-bath, along with a room for cooling and dressing.

The house is certainly impressive. Built on a rocky crag high above the Debdon Burn, Cragside Estate extends to a thousand acres. Lord Armstrong and Lady Margaret personally oversaw much of the garden's construction and planting. There are seven million trees, plants and shrubs, forty miles of walks and five lakes. Further away from the house sits the power house and water wheel, used to pump water up the hillside to the formal gardens, whilst inside the power house sits the hub of the hydro-electric system. Despite the sniping of some critics, the house was considered one of the modern wonders of the age. Among the more notable visitors was the Prince of Wales, who on his trip to the north-east in 1884 was an honoured guest of Lord and Lady Armstrong. The Prince arrived with Princess Alexandra and their three daughters. They were welcomed by a spectacular display of lights, which Lord Armstrong had hidden among the trees throughout the estate.

I'm no expert, but it certainly looked impressive to me. The style has been variously described as Wagnerian, Gothic and High Victorian. To my eye it looked like a Bavarian castle with a touch of Merrie England. Inside, the Grand Hall is the central showpiece, but many of the rooms are quite compact and really rather homely. In typical Victorian style, every corner of the house seems to be stuffed with paintings, books, photographs and ornaments. It must have been a nightmare to dust! There was barely a square inch that wasn't utilised. I later found out that the smaller rooms were in fact the original lodge which had been cleverly absorbed into the new build – a sort of house within a house.

Returning to the garden, it's not hard to see where Cragside gets its name from. The rock gardens are vast and hugely impressive. I'm not sure how much of the setting is natural and how much was dragged into position by Lord and Lady Armstrong. Whatever the mix and the input, the end result is very appealing. I'm still not sure about the twelve quid entrance fee though! It strikes me as a strange paradox that while the country's museums have been throwing open their doors, enticing the populace by dropping or abolishing entrance fees, the National Trust seems hell-bent on levering everything in sight up to a tenner plus. The amount of support they must now be receiving by way of grants, wills and general donations, I think a change of name is overdue. Maybe 'The National Truss' would be more appropriate?!

Throughout history the general consensus seems to have been, if you want to impress, build on a grand scale. If you want to create an air of mystery or spiritual presence, then place your structure on a high point of the landscape. And if there is an estuary to cross – so much the better. This is exactly what they did at Lindisfarne or as it is more commonly known, Holy Island. Like St Michael's Mount in Cornwall or Mont Saint Michel in Brittany, the moment you view them across a rugged causeway or see them set in glorious isolation on the incoming tide, you know you just have to visit them.

So this was it, Holy Island. On a pleasant day such as today, the castle high on the island mount looked enchanting, almost fairytale-like. The tide was receding and the island grew visibly larger by the minute as the water slipped away from its rugged shores, exposing the never-ending causeway.

I parked up and stopped to read a nearby sign. Once again, the National Trust had got to Holy Island before me. But this time there was not only a note of the charges, but a rather detailed sign explaining the somewhat complex details for your intended visit. It read thus:

> *Holy Island can only be reached by vehicle or on foot via a 3 mile causeway, which is closed from two hours before high tide until three hours after. Tide tables are listed in local newspapers, on the Northumberland County Council website and displayed at the causeway. To avoid disappointment check safe crossing and castle times before making a long/special journey. No large bags, pushchairs or rucksacks in castle. Emergency WC only; otherwise nearest WC in village 1 mile from castle. Admission £6.30* (a positive bargain by recent NT standards.)

I particularly liked the reference to emergency when describing the use of the toilet facilities. To my mind, what could so easily start off as an everyday call of nature could very soon turn into an emergency if you had to hike a mile or so to the nearest loo. Honestly, does anybody ever read these signs before agreeing to launch them on the poor unsuspecting public?

Holy Island, you may have gathered, is only accessible across a causeway at low-tide. Among its varied attractions are the ruins of the Benedictine Priory, which was among the many monasteries destroyed by Henry VIII. In fairness to Henry, he was – even if unintentionally – one of the country's first recyclers, as the stone from the Priory was used to great effect in building the castle high on the hill. Holy Island – still often referred to by its more ancient name of Lindisfarne – is accessible from the mainland village of Beal via two routes. A series of stakes mark the old route; this is known as 'Pilgrims Way' and was used in earlier times by visitors to the great Christian centre of Lindisfarne. To the south, the second crossing is a modern, surfaced roadway.

After an enjoyable hour's stride I reached the Snook on the western side of the island, which in turn led to the pretty Holy Island village. After a re-spiriting swift half at the Ship Inn, followed by the obligatory survey of the Celtic Craft and National Trust shops, these feet were off to view the castle. I even resisted the temptation to buy a parchment-style verse by Walter Scott.

> *For with the flow and ebb, its style*
> *Varies from continent to isle;*
> *Dry shood o'er sands, twice every day,*
> *The pilgrims to the shrine find way;*
> *Twice every day the waves efface*
> *Of staves and sandelled feet the trace.*

Built in 1570–2, as previously stated, with the stone nicked from the nearby Abbey, the castle sits on Beblowe Craig – a volcanic mound and the highest point of the island. Originally built to safeguard an important harbour providing shelter for English ships at war with Scotland, it was robustly built to withstand any siege. Following the accession of James VI of Scotland to the English throne in 1603, and the subsequent uniting of the two kingdoms, Lindisfarne Castle lost its importance as a border fort. It's fair to say that, apart from one minor skirmish in 1715, when it was grabbed by the Stuarts (never a pleasant experience), then quickly retaken by the English, the castle never actually witnessed a major battle, although a small garrison was maintained at the fort up until the late 19th century. In later years – 1901 to be precise, Edward Hudson (founder of *Country Life* magazine) negotiated its purchase from the crown, and in 1902–3 he appointed none other than the famed architect, Sir Edwin Lutyens to oversee its conversion into a private dwelling. By 1968 the wonderful rooms created for Edward Hudson by Luytens lay empty and the castle was taken over by the National Trust - the nice people who were about to relieve me of another six and a half quid.

If you were looking for a unique place to live, then they certainly don't come any more unusual than this. The approach to the castle is via a winding pathway with the castle sitting perched and embedded into the rock summit. Both the position and the views are dramatic, yet in a perverse way utterly tranquil. Lutyens however managed to convert the unusual arched ceilinged rooms from cold unforgiving spaces to something approaching an Edwardian Gentleman's retreat. Though not to my particular taste, the rooms are homely, and I could imagine they totally suited the escapist nature of their former owner.

Across a rugged grassy area sits the small but impressive garden, laid out by Gertrude Jekyll in 1911. Just an eighth of an acre in size, it makes up for any lack of stature by the superb array of plants and their riotous colour. Gertrude had worked with Lutyens on several other country houses, and she adopted her country garden style for Lindisfarne. She approached the creation of her gardens in the same way an artist would their palette. Her main concern was always to create a sympathetic blend of colour and pattern. She was famed for grouping plants which on first sight would be thought not quite in harmony but the end results were always, in essence, garden sculpture. Viewed from the castle the walled garden is an attractive distraction; viewed at close quarters it is magical and in a strange sort of way sits in complete harmony with its rugged surroundings.

Lindisfarne (particularly the castle) was the setting of Roman Polanski's 1966 film *Cul-de-Sac*, starring Donald Pleasance and Lionel Stander. The film was shot entirely on location here. The island was semi-fictionalised into 'Lindisfarne Island' and they renamed the castle 'Rob Roy' (don't ask). The village itself didn't feature in the film; it was replaced by odd looking sheds made from half-sectioned, upturned fishing boats. I have a vague recollection of this film, and remember it even then some years after it was made, as somewhat odd. Then again most films that Donald Pleasance featured in, or Roman Polanski directed, could so easily fall into that category.

Time and tide were beckoning, but I gauged there was still enough time left to view the weird remnants from the Polanski film. I took one last look at the castle and made off down the precipitous slope towards the sprawling island sands. I could see the attraction of leaving these turtle-like shacks in situ, but were they now used as a northern version of the Brighton beach hut or a welcome refuge for homeless travellers? I have no idea. The long sandy pathway leading from the island is broken at set intervals by what appeared at first sight to be high viewing platforms, but were actually safety gantries in case you mistimed your crossing. Something I was determined not to do, as the thought of several hours perched high above an incoming tide held little appeal.

Where's Hadrian?

Following a rather uncomfortable night spent in a meagre guest house run by a hatchet-faced, old harridan who should have been roasted on a slow spit decades ago for running such a bloody miserable establishment, I set off in a rather grumpy state of mind – my destination: Hadrian's Wall. I had not intended to stop off at Hexham, but I was drawn siren-like to its obvious charms by a large brown and white road sign that stated: *Visit Historic Hexham and lose yourself in its ancient charms and welcoming people.* Well, the last part of the sentence wasn't actually on the sign, but it was exactly what awaited me in wonderful Hexham.

Hexham sits approximately twenty miles west of Newcastle and is the largest town in West Northumberland. Accessed from the A69 Newcastle to Carlisle road, it sits on the banks of the River Tyne. There has been a settlement here since Saxon times and during its long and somewhat chequered history the name has evolved from Hutoldesham to Hestoldesham, Hextoldesham and finally Hexham. In 1571, Hexham was incorporated into the county of Northumberland and became an ecclesiastical peculiar of the Diocese of York. Hexham has a wonderful Abbey church, rebuilt in the 12th century. The town has a lovely compact feel to it with meandering streets connected by darting alleyways that seem to beckon you on to your next mystery vista.

Among its many charms, one building in particular caught my

eye. Part way along the main street sat what had once been the 'Old Pharmacy'. Founded in the reign of William IV, its main façade was painted in a wonderful combination of crimson and black with partially frosted windows. Above the main entrance an impressive gold and black Royal Warrant added to the obvious grandeur of a time since passed. Sad to say, the pharmacy was no more. In its place stood a Poundstretcher store. Still at least the shop sign was finished in a subtle red to match the period exterior – so it's not all bad then. Hexham also has a delightful Caffé Nero, which is exactly where I was now off to. Following yesterday evening's episode, I felt in need of some comfort and some good coffee. Sleeping in a bed designed for Ronnie Corbett and having more loose springs than Zebedee does very little to lift the morning's spirits, but Nero certainly helped restore my naturally happy demeanour.

Prior to James VI of Scotland becoming King, the border between England and Scotland was governed by appointed wardens. Their task – to maintain law and order and keep the marauding Scots at bay. The border was divided into three marches and Hexham was the headquarters of the Middle March. It's also home to the oldest purpose-built gaol in the country. I was busy viewing the exterior of this building when a charming lady coaxed me inside to uncover its history. I must admit that had it not been for her intervention, I may have passed this one by. It was, after all, not the largest place I had come across on my travels. I was chewing over the admission price in my mind, when she pounced. "You really should come in and have a look! It's well worth it, it's the oldest gaol in the country and the way they have set it out is very informative."

Well that was it – the next thing I knew I was stood looking at the stout, inner stone walls and wondering where the glass-sided elevator led to. My helpful guide Hilary informed me that Hexham gaol was built between 1330-3 by the then Archbishop of York, William Melton. Its principal inmates were by and large inhabit-ants of Hexhamshire awaiting trial at the nearby Moothall Court

Rooms. Because the sessions were only held every three months, your pre-trial stay could be either very short or perilously long. How little things change when you view first-hand an historic site such as this. For even as far back as the 15th century you either got the justice you could afford, or bought your level of comfort until you got the justice you could afford. Unlike today's prisons where your stay is paid for by the state, in this small stone tower your quarters were determined by how much you could afford – the elite on the top floors, and in descending order, the less well-off, and so on until you reached the free area – the dungeon. Here in a space no larger than a standard modern-day living room, up to thirty wretched souls were kept in dark, damp and totally insanitary conditions. Very often these poor people were innocent, their plight made none the easier by knowing that on the top floor some lucky sod was biting into a ham shank and quaffing mead.

"Take the lift to the basement area," said Hilary, "you can't get out, but it will give you an idea of just how cramped the prison area was. After that, simply press the button for whichever floor you wish to view. If you have any questions afterwards I will be more than happy to answer them for you."

I descended the short distance in my glass box, my goodness she was right, how did thirty or so people survive in such a cramped area? The lift was preset to spend a limited time at this level before requesting your next floor. The next obvious stop was the top floor, to see how the well-set miscreants faired. I can tell you without reservation, it was a bloody sight different than the folks on ground-minus-one. On this floor there was a wide fireplace and windows to reinforce your view that some form of life still existed outside these grim walls. At this level your food was probably brought in by a comely wench of your staff or at least a buxom young gal from the local hotel! The floors in between were given over to various displays depicting the importance of this border town and its history of border skirmishes – honestly, these Scots!

Back on the ground floor, I chatted at length with Hilary, a charming young lady who had left the comfort of friends and family in Hertfordshire some fifteen years ago, and was now almost accepted as a local – almost! She waxed lyrical about the area in the way only a person with a fresh perspective on an area can.

"The countryside is glorious and the people so friendly, here you become part of the community rather than a number. I have everything I want here and Newcastle is no more than a half-hour's drive."

Not the way I came it's not. I thanked Hilary profusely and promised I would forward a copy of the upcoming book on that fateful day of publication.

I wandered back in the direction of the cathedral, but my access was barred due to a service in progress. So off to 'The Wall' I went. Hilary had kindly told me that the best way to view Hadrian's handiwork was 'via the old road that runs parallel to the wall and known locally – not surprisingly – as Wall Road'. This entailed a short drive in a northerly direction, through the village of Wall (how imaginative is that?), before taking a left turn onto the old Carlisle Road.

Hadrian's Wall commenced construction around AD 122 following a visit by the Roman Emperor Hadrian. Measuring approximately eighty Roman miles, it is believed to have taken around six years to build. Britain was proving difficult to rule due in no small part to the efforts of, among others, the marauding Scots (or as they were then known – the Northern Tribes). Keen to impose order upon this 'island race', he decreed that 'the power of Rome was absolute, and must be upheld'. The wall was thought to have been originally constructed to prevent small groups of cattle raiders and antagonists, not so much a fighting line as a permanent barrier, making any attack extremely difficult. The Emperor reduced his military presence in the territories between the Tyne and the Humber, and instead devoted all his efforts to constructing this unique landmark. 'The Wall' eventually replaced Stanegate Road as the natural border of the Roman Empire.

Well, my friend at Hexham gaol was spot on: this was the best way to view Hadrian's Wall. For mile upon mile the road skirts the great stone structure, dipping down into steep valleys then rising to wonderful summits once protected by impressive forts. It was easy to see why the Emperor chose this natural ridge to watch the fearsome hoards from 'or'e the borda'. My first stop was Brunton Turret. Built by the men of the 20th Legion, it is approximately seventy yards long and one of the best-preserved turrets on the line of Hadrian's Wall. From here it was but a short walk until you had an uninterrupted view across the miles of open country, ensuring advance warning of any unwelcome visitors and plenty of time for a quick snifter before engaging the enemy. In an age less preoccupied with conservation and more concerned with the day-to-day hardships of life, over the centuries the locals have systematically removed great tracts of the wall to provide shelter for both themselves and their animals. Still there was enough of the fort left to get a clear indication of its size, and very impressive it must have been. The road hugs the wall for mile upon mile, and as you drive along you begin to realise the enormity of its construction. I suspect the average civil engineering company would perform cartwheels if they were commissioned to build a 21st century equivalent. I stopped off at regular intervals along the way, and each new vista seemed just as spectacular as the previous one.

The time was pushing 2.30pm as I pulled up at one of the many parking spots that adjoin the wall. Sitting on a two thousand year old construction must rank as one of the more unusual locations for lunch, but the sun was warming and with little sign of any Tartan invaders to spoil my repast, I tucked into a delightful ham salad baguette and took in the open views. It's a peculiar sensation to think that the place where I sat had once been guarded by an Italian in a heavy skirt and leather sandals!

They say you can't have too much of a good thing. Actually you can, and this was turning out to be one of those moments. Don't get me wrong, I think the wall is quite spectacular, and everyone should visit it at least once in their lifetime – it's just that it stretches out for mile upon never-ending mile, and once you have peeked over it and admired the view, visited a fort or two and had lunch on it, there is very little else to say – except farewell.

A Forgotten Port

Drive directly from Hadrian's Wall and Carlisle in a westerly direction, and you skirt the top of Cumbria. Here, where the Lakes end and the hills roll ever nearer to Scotland, the scenery is less dramatic; the villages less populated and the places less visited. Nestling at the entrance to the Solway Estuary is the coastal town of Maryport just as the sign so succinctly stated: 'Maryport – Near the Lakes, by the Sea'. Originally established as the Roman fort of Alauna around AD 122, it served as a supply base for the coastal end of Hadrian's Wall. There was also a substantial fort here to deter the clever Scots crossing the Solway Firth. Like the area itself, the fort became less important with the passage of time. Race forward to the Georgian era and the actions of a local landowner named Humphrey Stenhouse. Gaining an act of parliament to create his vision of a fine 'Georgian Town and Port', Humphrey set about his task. One of his first changes was the name of the area, which was changed from Ellenfoot to Maryport in honour of his wife Mary.

Standing in Maryport's Fleming Square it is easy to see the influence of this forward-thinking man. The buildings are lofty and impressive, and although the influence is obviously Georgian, its cobbled sectioning and central obelisk lends a strangely continental feel to it, appearing more like Normandy than Cumbria. Once again it appears that Stenhouse was determined to immortalise his wife's presence – the square is named after his wife Mary's maiden name.

I didn't dig any further for fear that all the streets had been named after their offspring – eg Rupert Street, Alice Gardens, Cuthbert Crescent etc.

It wouldn't be me if I didn't manage to unearth the odd fact or two about the places I visit, and there is no better place to dig into the unexpected than the local museum. I find it's the smaller, less pompous places that throw up some of the best anecdotes and history. I suppose when you don't have the Elgin Marbles or similar to fall back on, you find your history and interest where you can. In this respect, Maryport Maritime Museum was a classic.

Among the more notable sons of this small port, was none other than Fletcher Christian of HMS Bounty fame, who sailed from Maryport to the Pitcairn Islands – some stride indeed! Along one wall were numerous pictures and photographs of the SS *Titanic*, the connection becoming less obtuse when I realised that Thomas Ismay, the founder of the White Star Line – owners of this infamous ship – was also a Maryport boy. It's also documented that a regular visitor to this town was the author Charles Dickens, who would stay at the farmhouse that is now the Golden Lion. So there we have it, within the space of two rooms I had read about a shipping magnate, an author and a mutineer. This looked promising!

In the mid-1800s, the Elizabeth Stenhouse Docks (there's that name again) were opened, principally to ship coal to Ireland. This was followed by the Maryport to Carlisle railway, which opened in 1845. The rail link created by George Stephenson helped to make Maryport the largest dock in Cumbria. A period of roughly eighty years of prosperity ensued before the inevitable downturn came. By 1927 the game was up and Maryport slid into a gradual decline.

Over the next sixty years or so Maryport became a 'Forgotten Port'. Although against all odds its small fishing industry managed to survive, and to this day is still very much a working fishing port. The various craft unload their catches daily and much of it is sold in the local shop, aptly named The Catch. I stood on the quayside watching the fishermen attending to the maintenance of their boats. A gent of senior years stood in similar idle fashion watching the boys below. "Thes not a patch on the numbers es yoos te de this"

"Pardon?"

"Thi's no but a fraction of the men now as when I grew up."

"What, the fleet was a lot larger?"

"Larger, I'll si, when they were in from the Solwi Fith, thi couldn't see the end of em, just boat upon boat and men everywhere, they used to queue ti git in thi pubs." His eyes seemed distant as he nostalgically relived the scene.

"Not everything in life improves with time, does it?" I replied.

"Far from it lad, far from it."

I found his conversation enjoyable on two levels: for the obvious knowledge he had to impart, but more importantly, the fact he called me lad! Based upon his observations, I took it that there obviously wasn't a branch of Specsavers within a twenty-five mile radius of Maryport.

Since its economic low point, this pretty Cumbrian town has relaunched itself as a very pleasant tourist destination. I walked across to Maryport's rather impressive new Marina stood under a near cloudless sky surrounded by the sound of tinkling halyards. With the Lakeland Fells to one side, the Solway Firth and the Scottish hills on the other, it wasn't hard to spot the appeal. If all this were not enough, each year in July this little town hosts a world-renowned blues festival. Looking at the geographical location of Maryport you would not have selected it for an international event, but you are not Maryport Developments Ltd. The town at this time was receiving substantial regeneration grants from the EU and others. The stroke of genius here was to realise that new buildings alone don't make for a new public spirit. Maryport Developments Ltd were wise enough to appoint a separate company to oversee what was in essence a major gamble, and so they sub-contracted the promotion and organization of the festival to Albion Management Ltd. By 2003, with development money drying up, it was obvious that something more permanent had to be in place if the festival was to continue. On May 28th 2003 Maryport Festivals Ltd was incorporated. The key directors were by and large experienced festival volunteers, and so the foundation for a secure future was established. Each year in excess of 130 volunteers put in some 5000 man hours to ensure its continued success, attracting such luminaries as John Mayall, Van Morrison, Ruby Turner and the Blues Band with Paul Jones. People now travel from all corners of the globe to attend this three-day, mid-summer event. I think we can safely say that Maryport is no longer 'A Forgotten Port'.

The Train on Platform One

This close to the Lake District you can almost guarantee the weather will be extreme. You are either going to be caught in a deluge and blown sideways or toasted to a crisp. I have never yet visited this area on a temperate day but maybe I've just visited at the wrong time of year. Today was the first extreme: there was a brooding grey sky, swirling mist and drizzle that seemed as though it would never end. No wonder Wordsworth 'wandered lonely as a cloud', because no one with a less artistic temperament would be walking about the hills on a day like this.

Carnfoth sits in the north-west corner of Lancashire, just below Silverdale and inland from the Bay of Morecambe. It's not officially in the Lake District National Park but it's still close enough to share all their varied weather patterns. Many of the place names around this area are thought to have originated from the Danish invasion. Certainly some of the villages bear the Scandinavian influence in their titles - Thrang End, Hallgarth and Grisedale have little Saxon feel to them. Though the origins of Carnforth itself are not directly linked to the spear-carrying men in Longboats, it is in fact a derivative of the name Cherenforde, which referred to its position as a crossing point on the River Keer.

Surprise, surprise! By the time I parked my car on Market Street in Carnforth the sun had come out to play. Well not exactly play, more darting in and out of cloud, but it had stopped raining and was pleasantly warm – and that was good enough for me. The population of this market town had in earlier times been recorded as especially low. This was obviously not the case now – it had a very tidy and homely feel to it and the population was obviously now large enough to support a medium sized out-of-town Tesco. Always such a joy, particularly as this creates a number of clear glass shop windows in town, ideal for seeing first-hand the architectural merits of an empty Victorian shop or two. I wandered over to Carnforth Station and headed via the subway to the middle platform and the home of the much acclaimed visitor centre. Would you believe it – for once in my life I was actually early. I had arrived in the town around 9.10 am almost an hour before the centre opened at ten. One of the period-style posters that adorned the wall of the subway extolled the wealth of topics to be found at the Carnforth Bookshop, so being that I had the best part of an hour to kill, off I went. The modest façade of this local emporium belies the vast stock they carry; from local interest to transport, children's books to humour, and politics to poetry, they had the lot. Spread over two floors (upstairs was the second-hand department) and fourteen rooms, there had to be a book to suit every taste. I failed to select a book though; too many titles, too little time. I left the bookshop around 10.05am and strolled the short distance back to the station and the central platform. So this was it – the very station and platform made famous by the film *Brief Encounter*. I have to confess, this one was way before my time, but so were the Romans. It didn't mean that I couldn't be interested in a bit of social and cinematographic history.

When David Lean pitched up here in 1945 to direct a film version of Noel Coward's 1935 one-act play *Still Life*, he could barely have guessed at the enduring appeal this wartime filler would hold. Going on to produce such masterpieces as *Dr Zhivago*, *Lawrence of Arabia* and *A Passage to India*, this production couldn't have been more compact or less assuming if he had tried. Although he won critical acclaim for this work at the time, he must have dismissed its potency when set against the huge blockbusters he later directed. The town of Carnforth was chosen because all filming in and around the station had to be carried out between the hours of 10pm and 6am so as not to disrupt essential freight and troop movement. Carnforth was thought to be a safe distance away from any major industrial area, making it safer to light for evening work (less fear of attracting enemy aircraft). The station at this time had a further added bonus – a constant stream of fast-moving night freight trains, making it the ideal backdrop for those all-important action shots. Last but certainly not least, it had the long double-width, central platform and station buildings that were essential to the film's plot. It was well documented at the time that Celia Johnson was not looking forward to the filming, complaining: 'I will have to spend the next month or so in some dreary northern town or other'. Contrary to her initial misgivings, Celia found her time in Carnforth rather enjoyable, saying that 'the people she had met had been so sweet and kind, and made her very welcome'. How could she have ever doubted that it would have been anything else? Trevor Howard however was less easily pleased. Known to be rather aloof and quick to anger, he kept a rather lower profile than Celia.

Brief Encounter is a romantic drama set in 1945 during World War II. The principal action (if there is any action) is based in and around the fictional Milford railway station. Laura, a married woman played by Celia Johnson meets Trevor Howard's character Alec, a Doctor in the station's waiting room. The opening scene features the doctor gently removing a piece of grit from Laura's eye, before leaving to catch his train. During her regular shopping trips to Milford Laura meets Alec again and the friendship begins in earnest. As their relationship blossoms, both Alec and Laura find themselves falling in love. They regularly attend the cinema together and visit the surrounding area. The inevitable happens and they exchange kisses at the railway station. Whilst feeling the elation and joy found within these stolen moments Laura is always conscious that she is a married woman, so the feeling of guilt is never far away.

Laura continues the deception and after much soul-searching gives in to Alec's pleas and joins him at his friend Stephen's apartment, but Stephen returns unexpectedly to his flat and a guilt-ridden Laura runs away. Alec later catches up with her and breaks the news that he is soon to leave the country after receiving a job offer from his brother in South Africa. They meet the following week for a final rendezvous, enjoying a day in the country and one last romantic visit to the station's tea room. During their last brief moments before the arrival of Alec's train, they are joined by Dolly Messiter, a talkative friend of Laura who is soon inanely chattering away, totally oblivious to the couple's inner misery.

Realising that any chance of a passionate goodbye kiss has now evaporated, Alec's train arrives. After shaking Messiter's hand, he lightly squeezes Laura on the shoulder and leaves. Laura waits in the vain hope that Alec may return, but he doesn't. In the final scene the train is heard pulling away, Laura dashes out onto the platform, the lights of a passing express train flash across her face, and for a brief moment you wonder if she will take her own life. Dejected, she returns home to her family. That's the basis of this classic film, no swearing, no nudity, no violence, and yet sixty-odd years later it can still hold an audience.

The post-war demise of steam power and the radical cuts imposed by Dr Beeching in the 1960s led to the gradual decline of Carnforth Station. The mainline platforms were eventually closed and subsequently removed in 1970, prior to the electrification of the West Coast Main Line. Carnforth was downgraded to a branch-line station, and the buildings sadly fell into disrepair. The Carnforth Station and Railway Trust Co Ltd was formed in November 1996 for the sole purpose of restoring the now-derelict buildings. In late 2000, in co-operation with Railtrack, a £1.5 million restoration scheme was introduced. In 2003 the first fruits of all their collective hard work bore fruit, when the *Brief Encounter* Refreshment Room and Visitor Centre was opened on 17th October.

Housed within the whole of the central platform buildings, the results are outstanding. There are crisp black and white photographs of both cast and crew at work on the set of the film; detailed descriptions of the filming process and original letters and instruction notes. In addition, one central room is given over to a large-screen TV, which features the film on a continuous play loop. There are approximately twenty or so chairs set out in this viewing area. The audience this morning was an organised party of some sort. Curly-permed, white-haired ladies, who sat entranced by the film accompanied by the odd husband who seemed more interested in the pictures of steam trains that adorned the walls than any film. I stood to the rear of the ladies and watched the television for ten minutes or so. I didn't get it. The voice of Celia Johnson was so clipped and the whole film so angst-ridden that it was hard to believe that people actually did behave in such a structured way. I suspect that anyone under a certain age would lose the whole drama of the situation. The inclusion of Stanley Holloway as the jolly station master only added to the odd feeling of the film. Though I am probably being very unkind to the obvious fans of this much-vaulted film, so I will say no more.

As if to disprove my every theory, the guest book was positively gushing in its praise:

Fantastic.

Wonderful.

Thank you for keeping it all alive.

One lady from Dorset had written: *Still makes me cry!*

I presumed she was alluding to the film.

Despite any misgivings I may have had about the film, the actual visitor centre is a triumph. The tea rooms have been recreated to match the one featured in the film, complete with a steaming hot water geyser, period counter and very forties furniture. You can take a sneak peak at the station master's office used by Celia on cold nights between takes, where she was fortified by the odd brandy and convivial company of the true stationmaster. There is also the obligatory gift shop, stuffed with *Brief Encounter* memorabilia from postcards to posters. The efforts of the volunteers has given new life to what was once a derelict and forgotten piece of cinema history. In addition, they have provided a wonderful environment for the regular users of this line. Don't forget that this is still a valid stopping point! Just to complete the whole experience you can step back onto the platform and have your photograph taken under the circular clock.

This huge timepiece was made in the late 19th century by Joyce of Whitchurch. Now fully restored, it hangs above the subway entrance and being a completely mechanical clock is wound by hand every seven days. If all the splendid work and continuing effort were not enough, the icing on the cake is that the whole experience – with the exception of the refreshments – is free. Ladies and gentleman of Carnforth Station Visitor Centre – I salute you, and rest assured, your place in heaven is secure.

I left Carnforth with a happy disposition and headed for Silverdale and Arnside. I drove through winding lanes and stretches of road that resembled a fairground ride at times, as they descended towards Silverdale in a series of rolling humps – great fun! There is little to see at Silverdale except the never ending Bay of Morecambe as it stretches out towards Grange-over-Sands and the Lake District. I parked up at Silverdale, and for the next hour or so walked the headland in the direction of Arnside. Still with little more to see and a very tame pathway, I accepted Silverdale for what it was – a dot on the map.

Back in the car I pressed on to Arnside. Passing through Yealand Conyers where everything was constructed of random grey Lakeland stone: the houses, the walls, garages, church and school – everything. What it looked like on a miserable winter's day I shudder to think, but under a brightening summer sky it was delightful. Although strangely there wasn't a soul in sight – maybe they were made of stone too? It wasn't enough to pass through Yealand Conyers; I had to pass through Yealand Redmayne and Slack Head before eventually pitching up at Arnside.

Sat in the comfort of my car, I munched away at a 'custard rollover' (I know, great name isn't it?) and sipped at my takeaway tea, all courtesy of the local bakery, the sort of place that bakes its own bread and cakes and where you really wouldn't mind if they accidentally locked you in for the night. I opened the road atlas looking for what I had thought was a road crossing to Grange-over-Sands. As I found out when I asked a friendly local if I could walk over to Grange, it wasn't.

"You can if you want, but I don't think the railway people would take very kindly to it – it's a rail track."

"Whoops – thank you."

"You could walk round the headland. It's a hell of a trek mind. If I were you I'd catch the train – there's one due in about fifteen minutes, and it only takes about three minutes to Grange-over-Sands."

Do you know? He was spot on.

In no time at all I was stood on the platform at Grange-over-Sands. The station is a little gem, all glass canopies and wrought-iron pillars, pristine in every degree, right down to the cast-iron benches with their ornate squirrel reliefs.

From here I could see… guess what?

That's right, Morecambe Bay, but the reverse shot of what I had viewed from so many angles all day – and it's just as big from this side. Grange-over-Sands sits around a swooping bay and is dotted with fine Edwardian, limestone houses. Once the preserve of the well-heeled of Cumbria, they now play host to tourists as comfortable hotels and guest houses. I don't want to appear ageist or anything, but half the population of this sleepy town looked at first glance to be somewhat frail. Those who weren't walking with the aid of a stick or a walking frame were slowly progressing in cars along the main street at a breathtaking 4mph, or zipping about the pavement at 20mph on mobility scooters. They really are lethal those things! I immediately felt like a young lad who'd just popped in to see the grandparents. After strolling along the seafront and pressing my nose against a few shop windows, I decided to move on. I had nothing against Grange, it's just that there were other places to investigate, and this place felt like Dorian Gray in reverse.

You may have noticed by now that I have somehow dodged the bulk of the Lake District; in my travels this is a deliberate omission on my part and here's the reason why:

Alfred Wainwright was born in Blackburn in 1907, the son of a stonemason. He left school at the age of thirteen to start work as an office boy in Blackburn Borough Engineer's Department. Alfred was twenty-three before he made his first trip to the Lake District. From this point on he would return to the hills when time allowed. A diligent and quiet man, he studied hard to pass his exams and subsequently became a municipal accountant. In 1941 he applied for and was chosen for a position in the Borough Treasurers Office in Kendal. His love for all things Lakeland was now evident and around this time he started his now-famous pen and ink drawing of the fells. Each weekend he would venture out onto the fells, laying the basis for what was to become his *Pictorial Guide to the Lakeland Fells*. The works were printed in exactly the same flowing script and punctuated with his meticulous maps and drawings. Only recently has his true genius come to be fully appreciated. It is for this reason alone, that I have decided not to include the heart of the Lakes within this book. How can I begin to describe in four days, four weeks or even four years, what one man has devoted a lifetime to. I cannot compete, nor would I wish to.

My priority now was to find somewhere to rest my head for the night.

The White Hotel

I parked the car at Hest Bay and went for a stroll along the low headland. Looking across the bay to the Lakeland hills it was easy to see the danger that lay within this bay. When the tide is out, the mile upon mile of sand must be a temptation, even to experienced walkers. Off to Morecambe.

Twenty years or so had elapsed since I last drove into Morecambe. I confess, despite the obvious adverse publicity that this seaside town has received over the ensuing years, I was determined to view it with an open mind. Morecambe Bay was barely visible below a brooding sky that completely obliterated the Lakeland hills. The tide was in and the sea, a grey-green soup, lashed the harbour walls while the rain formed a horizontal sheet, making the walk by the sea wall just a little challenging. Eric Mitchell described Morecambe Bay, in his book of the same name, as 'a great inner sea, low tide reveals a tawny desert 120 square miles in extent. Crossing the Sands – and the estuaries of Keer and Kent – was once part of a daring west coast route linking Lancashire with its northern territory of Furness. It is certainly a dangerous place. Cast your mind back to 2004 when thirty Chinese cockle-pickers were cut off by the rapid incoming tide at Hest Bank, and you will recall just how dangerous. A massive rescue bid involving the RNLI, coastguards and the RAF was rapidly launched. Sadly sixteen men and two women lost their lives.

* * *

This is just the latest sad event in the rather daunting history of Morecambe Bay. The problem with this bay is that it is simply huge (174 square miles), with a tide that appears to swirl in from several directions at once, leaving many a distracted holidaymaker suddenly stranded on a sand barr. Any attempt to find your way back to shore can be easily thwarted by the quicksands. Morecambe has an official guide to the sands – a man who has spent a lifetime navigating this treacherous bay. When the tide is out, it is perfectly possible to walk the six miles across the bay to Cumbria and many do, but I for one wouldn't do it without a guide. I would choose someone like Frederic Robinson, who has walked the sands for over forty years, and tells some great tales of his years as a bay guide. In his own words:

"There was one chap who was determined to do the walk. Had we kept to the sand I think he would have made it. But the river moved and we had to make inland over Silverdale Marsh and he had a wooden leg. Once we got going over the marsh his wooden leg kept sticking. He had somebody with him but he was holding up the group – 150 of them. Because of the change of route it was taking us longer and you have to be at the river at pretty much the right time. I felt sorry for him, but we had to get transport for him. He was terribly disappointed."

I'd read several articles over the previous couple of years, telling of the concerted efforts to re-establish Morecambe as an alternative base for visitors to the Lakes; a sort of upmarket, weekend slot within easy driving distance of Kendal and the Lakeland routes. Optimism had been buoyed principally by the purchase and refurbishment of the lovely, seafront Art Deco hotel, the Midland. I'd once had the dubious pleasure of staying there. Even two decades ago, it had passed its best but there was still enough left of the old place to appreciate just what a wonderful place this must have been in its heyday. Now, thanks to the efforts of a Manchester development company named Urban Splash, the Midland can once again hold its 1930s head up high.

Walking along the seafront at Morecambe it is hard to miss this beacon of hope. This and the much loved statue of Eric Morecambe were sadly, as far as I could see, the only rays of light in what is being vaulted as Morecambe's resurgence. In common with most councils, Morecambe has carried out its own share of improvements (read 'destruction'). Though, sadly, not even the council and its planners could be held responsible for the downward slide of what is essentially a pretty town. Looking at Morecambe today, it is hard to believe that at the height of its popularity, it had in excess of 1,400 hotels and guesthouses. During the Lancashire Wakes Weeks, when the main mills and factories across the area closed as one, in excess of 90,000 people would descend on Morecambe. If Morecambe had to point the finger of blame anywhere, then the number one suspect would be Spain. The advent of the package holiday and the mass summer exodus to the Costas was the final act in Morecambe's slow death. Along with many other once-popular British resorts, it had no answer to the lure of two weeks' continual sunshine and cheap booze.

On this foulest of late summer days, I could see very little glimmer of hope for this jaded town. Despite the wide and pleasant promenade and the general cleanliness of the town, there was no getting over the look of hopeless desperation evident by the lack of quality shops and restaurants. And apart from the obvious improvement now on show at the Midland, no sign of the much talked of 'New Morecambe'.

The weather was doing its utmost to flatten any enthusiasm I may have found for this Lancashire resort, so I sauntered over to the Deco palace for a spot of lunch. I must say, this was a bit different from the last time I crossed the threshold. Smart and gleaming, the outer façade looked very similar to the one I remembered. Inside there was barely a room that hadn't been revamped. I was pleased to see they had retained the original wide spiral staircase and the wonderful circular ceilng panel by the renowned sculptor Eric Gill.

The original Midland Hotel opened on Wednesday 12th July 1933. The Earl of Derby toasted its success and complimented the LMS (this was a railway hotel) on providing a 'magnificent building, which set an example for others to follow'. Sir Josiah Stamp, President of LMS (don't you just love some of these names? If you were going to have a name for the head of a railway company, then Josiah Stamp is about as near-perfect as you can get) said he had recently seen the most up-to-date hotel accommodation in Chicago, Copenhagen and Stockholm, embodying the latest modernism, cubism and other 'isms' but the new Midland Hotel eclipsed them all.

The new hotel opened to widespread critical acclaim, *Architecture Illustrated* devoting an entire issue to the Midland. The Midland became an immediate success. With a plethora of stars appearing at the nearby Winter Gardens, the only place to stay when in town was the Midland. The guest list read like a Who's Who of bygone names: George Formby, Joe Loss, Harry Roy, Ambrose and many others played or stayed here.

I ordered a rump-steak burger and a glass of chilled house-white and watched through the new, gleaming, aluminium framed windows of the Rotunda Bar as the RNLI – who were holding their annual open day – demonstrated their prowess with flares by setting off several across the bay. This looked to be about the only brightness we were likely to witness in the skies over Morecambe today. Then almost as this thought had crossed my mind, the rain ceased and the outline of the hills appeared across the bay. The tide, now on its way out, revealed an impressive sandy beach stretching out around the bay. From this position Morecambe looked very pleasant. I spent a further half hour or so in the comfortable surroundings of the Rotunda bar before returning to the foyer, where, by kind permission of the young man on the reception desk, I took several photos of the hotel interior for the trip record.

I crossed the road to the huge Victorian, red-brick Winter Gardens, a one-time Moss Empire theatre, and past host to some of the biggest names in showbiz. Stars like Ken Dodd, Gracie Fields, The Goons and the Crazy Gang all headlined here. Sadly, like most of the attractions in this forgotten town, the Winter Garden's demise was slow and painful. It struggled on until 1977 when it was deemed unsafe for public use. Today there were several men in high visibility jackets and hard hats clambering over the first floor scaffolding, part of the slow, ongoing restoration of this Grade Two listed building. Threatened with demolition, 'The Friends of The Wintergarden' was formed, a charity committed to restore this fine building to its former glory. Thanks to them, the exterior of the building is now watertight and secure, its deep red brick façade cleaned and scrubbed, although the interior may take a little longer to return to pristine condition. I wish them well in their endeavours. The Winter Gardens certainly beats the horrific shopping arcade built a few scant years ago – a pathetic attempt to enrich the lives of locals and visitors alike. Honestly!

Despite the sad image presented thus far, I had the nagging doubt that I was being a little harsh on Morecambe. I had concentrated all my efforts on the south side of this town; there had to be more, perhaps I needed to look at the northern sector.

I walked back along the length of the promenade, passing Eric Morecambe once more – still they were taking their photos, snuggling up to his bronze replica. I couldn't help but think that Eric would somehow have loved this statue; it certainly strikes a chord with his fans, and all that visit him come away smiling.

The further north I progressed the nicer Morecambe became. I decided to venture a couple of streets back at this point, and what I found startled even me. This was pure gold. Street upon street of the prettiest stone cottages, delightful chapels and a wonderful high school. This was more like it; it reminded me more of a fishing village than a full blown seaside town. The place oozed potential. With just a little investment, a few good shops and nice restaurants, I believe Morecambe could turn that elusive corner.

It was time to move on. I wish I could say that Morecambe was on the way back, but somehow I can't see it. What Morecambe really needs is a way of creating some gainful employment or purpose for the local residents. This will only come, I feel, from direct intervention from government or big business, or both. Until that day this lost seaside town will, I fear, just struggle on.

I hadn't intended to stop off in Lancaster, but thanks to our old friends the town planners, I was stuck in a traffic jam outside this charming town. Let me expand a little on that last statement. The main road to Morecambe used to take a direct route through Lancaster. Now thanks to a well-intentioned by-pass, you are diverted via a peculiar strip of road that is totally inadequate for the volume of traffic. The one benefit, however, is that while you're stuck in this continual traffic chaos, you're afforded a view of Lancaster that few in the past, including myself, have ever seen. Across the wide River Lune, old warehouses and waterside buildings have been lovingly restored, giving a totally unexpected vista as you sit tapping your steering wheel – a more than welcome distraction, and one that found me parking my car in central Lancaster.

Lancaster is – if you don't already know – the county seat of Lancashire. The old town sits under the watchful eye of the very impressive castle, parts of which date back to 1150. Due to its strong strategic position, the castle and Lancaster area were entrusted to those closest to the throne. It became part of the Honour of Lancaster and the centrepiece of the County Palatine. When the third Duke of Lancaster, Henry Bolingbroke, came to the throne in 1399 as King Henry IV, the castle became part of the Duchy of Lancaster and so the owner is our current monarch, Queen Elizabeth II. From the late 18th century the castle was substantially modified for its use as a court house and prison and is still in use today.

The streets that sit below this impressive building are a joy. Thanks to the new relief road (not much relief for motorists), the town is virtually traffic-free, with pretty stone-built houses and shops that sit at peculiar angles off winding streets. There are retail outlets galore, and indicative of many tourist-driven places, the goods on sale never cease to amaze. From herbs to rocking horses and deep pink sheep-skins – Lancaster had them all. I'd always considered the centre of Lancaster to be rather quaint, but the outskirts were always rather depressing. In a previous era Lancaster had been the centre of a very impressive linoleum industry. As the industry slowly died, derelict factories and mills lay empty; the same had happened down by the River Lune. Once a thriving port, Lancaster had been the base for importation of rum, sugar, exotic timbers, hemp, flax and sadly, slaves. What really intrigued me was what they had done to the old warehouses and buildings along St George's Quay, so off I tootled to find out.

Well, haven't Lancaster Council, or whoever is responsible, done well. If ever there was a blueprint for imaginative and tasteful regeneration that will last well into the future, this is it. The old warehouses and quayside buildings have been sand-blasted and spruced up. And shining like a proud new pin, at the centre of all this renewed real estate, is the old Custom House, a grand Palladian-fronted treasure. What were once obviously derelict eyesores have been transformed into riverside apartments, and as so often happens with such major regeneration, the bars, pubs and shops had followed closely behind. The whole area felt energised and infectious in its obvious optimism. A final piece of foresight had been the addition of the Millennium Bridge. A stunning piece of grey steelwork that links St George's Quay to the Millennium Park and the village of Caton. Despite some strong opposition to this revolutionary bridge (it includes an unusual curved deck linking the old viaduct), strangely from some of the newer residents in the waterside apartments, the bridge was opened a year later than promised, in 2001. I personally think it's great!

Standing on Lancaster's newest landmark, I had a clear view of one of its more established ones. High on a hill in Williamson Park, overlooking Lancaster and clearly visible from the M6 motorway, sits the Ashton Memorial. Designed by John Belcher for Lord Ashton (formerly James Williamson), it is built of Portland stone and has a copper dome. Born in Lancaster, Lord Ashton became a millionaire producing linoleum. From the port of Lancaster he exported his product all over the world, and made himself a few quid into the bargain. The Folly was built by Lord Ashton as a memorial to his late wife.

I wandered back to St George's Quay and the stunning Customs House. Built in 1765 and now a maritime museum, it is the most perfect example of high Georgian architecture you could wish to see. Paying the very reasonable admission charge of £2, I went forth to investigate.

Any dateline was forgotten at the door, as the museum had set out with the sole intention of including anything nautical and relevant, whatever the period. There were small boats, known locally as coracles, an early canal boat and a couple of rooms set out as they would have appeared in Georgian times, one of them the collector's office. The latter, although a reproduction of the original, somehow still manages to feel quite threatening – most peculiar. I spent an enjoyable forty-five minutes or so reading the very informative tags and plates, before ending up at my favourite section of the Museum – the coffee bar.

With cappuccino in hand, I read through a few of the leaflets I'd gathered along the way. Sadly, the most interesting one was also the most gruesome topic – the slave trade. This was odd, I'd never thought of the slave-trade as being active any further than Liverpool, but here I was reading about a smaller but equally lucrative transportation of these wretched souls, here in the county seat of Lancashire.

The majority of the vessels used for this abhorrent trade were, shockingly, purpose built in Lancaster or Preston. Commonly known as brigs or snows, they weighed between twenty and seventy tons and were approximately fifty feet in length. These were relatively small ships, when compared to the ones that operated out of Liverpool and Bristol. Although this meant the ships could carry fewer slaves, they had the advantage of being ideal for navigating the Windward Coast, entering the River Gambia and traversing African estuaries where slavery was more specialist. In addition, these vessels were fast, so less time was spent along the African coast, thus reducing the potential risk to cargo and crew posed by tropical diseases. Usually crewed by local young men seeking adventure and a good wage, the vessels were financed by local merchants who would buy shares in the ship or the voyage. The more detailed accounts left me wondering why slavery took quite so long to abolish?

Returning once more to central Lancaster, I found myself in Dalton Square, a handsome little park, with a somewhat over-grand central statue of Queen Victoria – has anyone ever thought to count the number of monuments erected to this 'Little Lady'? If they did, I think we may all be surprised at the final count. I suppose Lancaster has more reasons than most to celebrate QV. This is, as previously mentioned, part of the Duchy, so by definition was her home. Donated by our old friend Lord Ashton in 1906, it has one peculiar detail – what appears to look like a hand holding the rear of the cloak. What the origins are, I have no idea.

Having spent the previous hours in Morecambe, I found it difficult to understand how two places so geographically close could be so far apart in their approach to regeneration. Here, Lancaster had done everything right. The project was measured, well-executed and, best of all, pleasing on the eye. In short they had looked at the wealth of good stock they possessed, and maximised its potential to the benefit of locals and tourists alike, whereas poor old Morecambe in the same decade had barely crossed the starting line – how sad.

Humour With Everything

I have visited Liverpool on more occasions than I can honestly recall. A good deal of those visits were spent promoting records and recording artists. I'd stayed at the Adelphi Hotel and a number of other pleasant hotels across Merseyside, normally at the expense of EMI records. If there was a concert taking place at the Floral Hall in Southport or the Guild Hall in Preston, it was down to yours truly and a couple of others to wave the company flag. This all sounds very grand, concerts, recording artists and receptions, until you realise that the vast majority of the artists performing within this area, were for some obscure reason, Country and Western stars. Manchester would have edgy new blood, Birmingham and London also – but if we were called to promote in Merseyside, nine times out of ten, it would be Country and Western. In one way this is not surprising, one of the many licensed record labels EMI pressed and distributed for at this time was Capitol Records, and a great deal of their catalogue happened to be Country and Western. The list of performers was endless – Glenn Campbell, Helen Reddy, Charlie Rich, Tammy Wynette, Merle Haggard, and a hundred other names I can't and don't wish to remember. Why Liverpool and its environs was so hooked upon this style of music I have no idea. Whether it was the Irish/Welsh influence or the maritime input, for example merchant seamen who in previous decades had brought back records from the United States, I couldn't in all honesty say. All

I can say with some authority is that the areas of Deeside, Liverpool, Birkenhead, Southport and Preston were unique in their love of the steel guitar, banjo and fiddle. When an album can realise its whole national sales target within one area alone, and normally within the first ten days of release, you don't ask questions – you just put on your checked shirt and get promoting.

All this brings me in a very convoluted way to my latest visit to Liverpool. For the reasons stated above, most of my visits to this city had to be by car, usually loaded to the gunwales with T-shirts, posters, pre-release or concert information and the whole circus that goes with any concert or record promotion. Unencumbered by anything more than a note pad, a camera and a pen, I elected to catch the train from Manchester Victoria to Liverpool Lyme Street. The trip into Liverpool was, I'm glad to say, totally uneventful. There were no bricks or concrete blocks thrown from a bridge by the mischievous, bored little angels, looking for some harmless fun as they welcomed visitors to their city (a practice that had been in the headlines too many times in recent years for my liking).

The moment you step outside Lyme Street Station you know you are in a city with a great past – that's not to say it doesn't have an equally great future, but the wide streets and the imposing façade of the St George's Hall let you know at once that this city was once Britain's second port and 'Gateway to the Empire'. In the late 19th century, Liverpool handled more goods than any other port outside London. Here is a proud city built upon great wealth and civic pride. Liverpool had, up until the 1950s, some of the finest Georgian and Victorian housing stock anywhere in Britain. I can fully understand that the devastation caused by wartime bombing and a desire to provide decent houses were paramount to Liverpool's planners, but as late as the mid-1980s I remember the feeling of complete bewilderment as I witnessed the random bulldozing of beautiful Victorian terraces, only to return in six months or so to see their inadequate replacements – utter madness.

That was two decades ago. I have visited the city on a couple of occasions in the intervening years, but each time Liverpool seemed to be in a state of flux, with either major roadworks making it impossible to move, or the constant sound of building work drowning any pleasure in the visit. I was therefore anxious to see if Liverpool had scrubbed up and presented itself to the wider world following its year as 'Capital of Culture'.

The city was busy, and on this pleasant summer morning (how lucky was I with this weather?) looked very impressive. I couldn't speak for the outskirts, but central Liverpool felt chirpy and very upbeat. I suppose when people have been telling you for decades that you are an ugly duckling, and you suddenly look at your reflection to find you have become, once again, a rather fine swan, you want to tell anyone and everyone who will listen – and Liverpool certainly appeared to be doing that. The rest of the UK may have fallen out of love with post-Beatle Liverpool for a time, but this never dented the Liverpudlians' collective ego; certainly, not as far as I could tell. I always remember them as being ultra-upbeat and always there with a quip, a pun or a joke. Once again, I have a theory: Liverpool was such a melting pot of cultures and influences, and life so utterly tough for the average working man, that the only defence left was the equivalent of gallows humour. This is never more evident than when you get a number of Scousers baiting someone from out of town. The humour is always ironic and self-deprecating, often black but seldom really cruel. Here are some examples:

Q. "Why wasn't Jesus born in Merseyside?"
A. "Because God couldn't find three wise men and a virgin."

Q. "Mummy, why are your hands so soft and smooth?"
(think of the Fairy Liquid commercial).
A. "Because I'm only fourteen."

And this gem told to me by an Everton supporter – I think they call it friendly rivalry:

> Q. "What's the difference between Pamela Anderson and the Liverpool goal?"
> A. "Pam's only got two tits in front of her."

> Four United States Presidents get caught up in a tornado, and are whirled off to the land of OZ and the Emerald City, where they meet the great Wizard.
> "Tell me, what brings the four of you before the great Wizard of Oz?"
> Jimmy Carter steps forward timidly: "I've come for some courage."
> "No problem," says the Wizard. "Who's next?"
> Richard Nixon steps forward: "Well, I think I need a heart."
> "Done," says the Wizard. "Who comes next before the Great and Powerful Oz?"
> Up steps George Bush: "The American people say that I need a brain."
> "No problem," says the Wizard. "Consider it done."
> Finally, up steps Bill Clinton and just stands there, looking around but doesn't say a word.
> Irritated, the Wizard finally asks, "Well, what do you want?"
> "Is Dorothy here?"

See what I mean? There is always a large dose of irony in a Scouse quip. Some years ago I spent several weeks in Liverpool, over a three-month period. The hardest thing to get used to was the constant banter. None of it was nasty, but when even the smallest request was met with a pun or a clever statement, it can become a little wearing.

Sadly for a time it seemed as though the joke was on Liverpool. Their low point came at the beginning of the 1980s when, along with Brixton in London and Moss Side in Manchester, major riots broke out in the city. With the country's unemployment figures spiralling out of control and places like Liverpool's Toxteth taking more than its fair share of the economic meltdown, discontent turned to anger. The young and not-so-young went on the rampage.

When the fires were extinguished 'the Bitch in Blue' decided she would have to send a representative of the Government to soothe the baying mob. Who did she call on to ride into the 'fires of hell', or at least Toxteth? None other than the 'Blonde Bombshell' – Michael Heseltine. Possibly this had been an act of callous sacrifice by Margaret Thatcher, a way to silence a very vocal cabinet member: 'oh! Lets send the posh boy in and watch while the scousers chew him up'. If so, it backfired spectacularly on her. Heseltine had the perfect touch – enough concern for Liverpudlians to believe that something could and would be done, matched by a no-nonsense attitude to doubters in the government and Home Counties. Not surprising really when you are talking of a man who once grabbed the mace in Parliament and shook it above his head in anger – earning him the nickname of Tarzan. You have to wonder what the outcome of the leadership challenge against Margaret Thatcher would have been if the population had been aware that John Major was in the habit of popping out for a quick Curry on a regular basis. Heseltine was as good as his word and many believe he laid the foundation stones of Liverpool's regeneration that, combined with ditching the far left element so prevalent at that time within the council chamber, meant a fresh start for this once great city.

I wanted to see just how far Liverpool had come, and there seemed no better place to start than down by the Mersey. The central area of the city has managed to pull off that delicate balancing act of keeping the best of the old while shoe-horning in the latest facilities. I'm not so sure about the much-acclaimed Liverpool One complex (another of Gerald Grosvenor's joint interests). I can see what they are trying to achieve by creating street precincts rather than the usual central block system of the 1970s – only time will tell if their efforts have hit the mark – but all in all the place looked very spick-and-span.

Crossing the wide dual carriageway that sadly separates the city from her waterfront, I arrived at probably Liverpool's most iconic landmark, the Liver Building, an impressive structure and widely referred to as one of 'the Three Graces' (sounds like a female pop group). Designed in 1908 by Walter A. Thomas and completed in 1911 for the Royal Liver Friendly Society, it was one of the first buildings in the country to use reinforced concrete on such a major scale. This 'new fangled construction' obviously worked, because it still looks as bright as a new pin with its twin towers topped by the Mythical Liver Birds. The birds are modelled on a cross between an eagle and a cormorant, made of copper, are eighteen feet tall and have a massive wingspan of twenty-four feet. Local legend has it 'if they fly away, Liverpool will cease to exist'. Personally, I think if these birds fly south, we're all stuffed.

The man responsible for creating such timeless sculptures was a German by the name of Carl Bernard Bartels. Although he had lived in England for some time, he was arrested at the outbreak of World War I and shipped off to the Isle of Man. Having once left Pier Head for a three-day business trip to the Isle of Man (and there's another story), I can vouch that the last thing Carl Bartels would have seen as the Packet Steamer left the Mersey estuary would have been his Liver Birds - how ironic is that?

The other two graces are the Cunard Building by Willinck & Thicknesse (what a great name), a stunning Art Deco pile, and the former offices of the Mersey Docks and Harbour Board by Briggs & Wolstenholme (1903-07). There were extensive plans for a 'fourth grace', originally planned to be in place by the time of Liverpool's 'Capital of Culture' year. Unfortunately, the detailed plans that followed an open competition for the design, the extensive consultation and outline planning came to nought. You could say it simply fell from Grace – sorry, but don't tell me you weren't thinking the same?

I had twenty minutes to kill before the next Mersey cruise so I decided to use the brand new facilities of the eaterie adjoining the departure terminal.

"Wot can I get ya?"

"I'll have a cheese and ham toastie and a coffee please."

I took my coffee and perched on a high stool overlooking Pier Head.

"Number seven!" – pause – "Number seven? Cheese an' 'am toastee."

Ah! Me, I think, I tucked into my toastie. This is a bit spicy – what cheese is this I wonder? Peeling open the sandwich, my cheese and ham had mystically turned into a peppered tuna sandwich.

"Sorry luv – bur it saays cheees an' 'am on the packet, we downt make 'em 'ere."

Most displeased and now out of time, I replaced it with a Danish and made for the ferry.

It's almost impossible to stand on a Mersey Ferry without humming the tune that takes its title from this stretch of water – *Ferry Across The Mersey*, made famous by Gerry Marsden. The fact that it was also playing at full tilt as I joined an assortment of nationalities for the trip along the Mersey Estuary didn't help. There was the usual mix of day-trippers from the UK, camera-wielding Japanese tourists (who seemed intent on snapping anything that moved, including me), a Spanish couple, small, dark and rather sombre and the obligatory Scot, whose impromptu rendition of the said song left a little to be desired. Then there was me, trying desperately to catch a little of the commentary above the intermittent music and the Hibernian yodeller.

The strange part of the whole Mersey Cruise was that it all felt so terribly familiar, the music only adding to the familiarity. I half expected Gerry Marsden himself to appear from behind the wheel house, strumming a guitar and lead us in a chorus of his anthem. I'd only ever left the UK mainland once from Pierhead and that was on a rough day in February as I took the Lady of Man steamer to Douglas on the Isle of Man. After a rather choppy crossing – that's nautical speak for twenty foot waves crashing over the deck – I was deposited in Douglas. After parking my car and dumping my kit and clobber at a rather cold and cheerless hotel, I ventured out on to the main promenade, only to discover that I was the sole visitor to the Isle of Man. Not a single soul was visible within half a mile in either direction and so it remained, more or less, for three long, dreary days.

I digress. What I was alluding to was – how many people had left these waters never to return? Families who in harder times had sought a new life in America and Australia (it's estimated that between 1815 and 1930, in excess of nine million people emigrated from this port). Then there were those serving in the merchant fleets of two wars, who had little choice in their departure, and sadly some who paid the ultimate price and never returned. What I'm saying is, this is a place that can heighten emotions even for an old cynic like me, so what it must have been like for those old salts who after months at sea caught their first sighting of the Liver Birds, I can only imagine. Knowing that pretty soon they would be downing a glass or two of Higson's best bitter in a familiar pub on the Scottie Road and no doubt telling a few new jokes. There has been a ferry service of some kind across these waters for in excess of six hundred years; the only difference being they didn't have Gerry Marsden singing in their ears.

In fairness, his intro didn't last too long, and the commentary was good. Good enough to inform me that by 1820 Liverpool was of such importance as a port that it was turning around over two hundred ships a week – that's right, two hundred plus vessels were unloaded and re-loaded every seven days. I found this figure quite staggering, and it set me thinking. Using a simple multiplier – two hundred ships a week, that's ten thousand ships a year, based on the fact that the average ship-length in 1820 was approximately eighty-five feet, had these vessels been placed end to end, this would equate to 161 miles of shipping per annum… just thought you'd like to know.

Despite the bright sunshine, out on the Mersey there was a biting wind and the temperature dropped alarmingly. A party of twenty or so schoolchildren had now joined us on the upper deck and, like the Japanese, they too were proving to be 'snappy happy', their preferred target not the Three Graces or the river views but the hovering seagulls, riding the thermals or whatever it is that seagulls ride.

I can't honestly say it was the most riveting hour I've ever spent. It was informative in as much as the Mersey harbour and estuary can be, as you chug along at a steady pace. The warehouses were warehouses and the container terminal now had four giant wind turbines, making it pretty much self sufficient in terms of energy, and that was about it on the Liverpool side. The trip towards Seacombe was far more pleasant; in particular, the New Brighton coast looked positively inviting in the bright sunshine – I planned to pop across later and have a look. The oddest part of the whole experience came after leaving the Birkenhead pier. The craft picked up an inordinate amount of speed and practically did a sideways drift on approaching Pier Head. As if to reinforce my earlier observations that Liverpool was now attracting people from far and wide, as I left the ferry approximately a hundred passengers were waiting to board. At a rough guess a good fifty percent of them were camera-wielding Japanese tourists. Liverpool really did feel very cosmopolitan. If they're still looking for a fourth grace, perhaps a giant statue of Michael Heseltine might be appropriate?

With the sun on my back, I strolled down Church Street towards three of Liverpool's most impressive public buildings – the Library, St George's Hall and the wonderful Walker Art Gallery. At the head of the stairs leading to the Walker's first floor gallery hangs a huge oil painting of Napoleon entitled *Crossing The Saint Bernard*, painted by Paul Delaroche. Napoleon is depicted on horseback leading his men across a snow-laden pass, the whole scene looking so desperately cold and unpleasant it's no wonder 'Old Bonie' has one hand stuffed well into his jacket. In the exhibition of *New Radicals: From Sickert To Freud* I was immediately drawn to a work by James Cowie (1886-1956), so utterly modern and simplistic that it reminded me more of a Russian revolutionary poster. The fact that it was painted decades before such influence only added to its obvious charm. I moved on to the Victorian Rooms and the Pre-Raphaelite Paintings. They were impressive but I have to say, and I know I risk the wrath of many an art critic here, when it comes to the Pre-Raphaelites, Manchester has the edge.

I crossed the square that fronts St George's Hall. So often the word 'awesome' is attached to places or things that are far from this descriptive term, but believe me this place is just that – totally awesome. It is built on such a grand scale that it would be hard to think of another municipal building within the UK that bears any comparison. The Hall is regarded as one of the finest examples of Neo-Classical architecture in the world; it's certainly one of the biggest, at one hundred and sixty-nine foot long and seventy-four foot wide. The foundation stone of the Hall was laid in 1838 to commemorate the coronation of Queen Victoria in the previous year, although it was a further five years before work commenced on this giant structure. It eventually opened in 1854, a multi-faceted building, housing a wondrous central hall-come-ballroom, concert arena and a criminal court. Following a major refurbishment (£23m), the hall was reopened to critical acclaim in 2007 just in time for the 'Capital of Culture' year.

This building has always been a focal point for the highs and lows of Liverpudlian life. When John Lennon was killed in December 1980, in excess of 25,000 people gathered outside St George's. Similarly, they packed the square in 2005 to welcome home their football club after they beat AC Milan in the Champions League Final. Once again, this time in 2008, 65,000 more Scousers gathered here to witness the opening ceremony for the 'Capital of Culture'. So I think it is fair to say that St George's Hall holds a very special place in the hearts of Liverpool people – and I for one can see why!

Just to cap it all, directly across the road sits the Liverpool Empire. The list of people who have trodden the boards here is vast, though probably one of the most memorable nights was November 8th 1964, when the Beatles played 'The Empire'. They were in the midst of a thirty-day UK tour. It is hard for anyone now to comprehend the complete hysteria witnessed at any Beatles concert. I was lucky enough to have a first-hand witness to this tour. One of the senior A&R guys at EMI records was appointed as their tour liaison manager. Harry (sadly no longer with us) regaled us with his first hand experience of the Beatles. By the time the show hit Liverpool, the boys had completed a US tour and this was the twenty-fourth date on their UK list. The Manchester show at the ABC Ardwick (now the Apollo) had been, Harry told us, complete mayhem. He and the boys had been smuggled out on the floor of a van. 'Nothing could have matched that'. How wrong could you be? Harry took his seat on the first balcony as the noise level was rising by the second. The story is best told in Harry's own words:

"I couldn't hear anything but a prolonged high pitched scream, then without introduction the curtain lifted and there stood the boys playing *She Loves You*, well, the place just erupted. It was impossible to hear the lyrics, the amplification was just about keeping pace with the decibel rate of the audience. Then the Beatles briefly said hello to Liverpool, and went straight into a rendition of *Love Me Do*. I kid you not, the stamping of feet was causing me serious concern that the balcony would not stand the strain. I swear it was bouncing. I have never before or since witnessed such scenes of collective hysteria."

So there we have it, I think the Boys went down well in the 'Pool.

Rapidly runing out of time, I decided I would leave Liverpool for today, so headed back to Lyme Street Station and Manchester Victoria. My return in the next day or so would be best served by car. Something told me there were still some more gems to unearth.

You know when you have seen or read something, that feeling of mild *déjà-vu*? Well, that's the way I felt about a man named Williamson and a series of rather odd tunnels that had been stumbled upon some years ago – more investigation was needed to dust off the old memory bank. This wasn't a figment of my imagination; there was a man of this name, and there was also a labyrinth of tunnels dug deep into the sandstone beneath the Smithdown Lane area of Liverpool.

Joseph Williamson was born 10th March 1769 near Darton in Yorkshire. The family then moved to Warrington. The earliest records suggest that when he arrived in Liverpool in 1780 to seek work, he was just eleven years of age. Liverpool was already a busy port, and he went to lodge with Mr Richard Tate and joined his tobacco company of the same name. When Richard died in 1787, his son Thomas took over the reigns of the company. Joseph rose through the ranks and in addition to his position with Tates, he joined forces with Joseph Leigh to set up a small company just yards away from the Tate office. In classic storybook plot, he married the current boss's sister Elizabeth in December 1802. Joseph was 33 years old. Around 1803, he purchased the tobacco company from Thomas Tate and the Leigh-Williamson partnership was incorporated within this established company – Joseph had arrived. In the same year the Williamsons moved into Mason Street – a house which was to be 'home' for the rest of their lives. Some time later he became the sole owner of the expanding tobacco company, so his wealth became assured. An ambitious man, he quickly set about building more properties nearby.

The area around Mason Street was at that time outside the city boundaries. In fact, it came under the jurisdiction of West Derby. Obviously a shrewd business man, Williamson bought the land that stretched from Mason Street to what is now the University of Liverpool campus. There was one problem to overcome though: the area was littered with open cast sandstone pits or quarries (more anon). Williamson's new homes were very grand affairs, built above the noise and mayhem of the city. Here high on a hill, you had uninterrupted views of the Mersey and little pollution or rowdiness to distract your comfortable existence. All the houses were built with cellars, and following the fashion of the day, Williamson also laid out large rear gardens; some even had small orchards. The land to the rear of these houses allowed a reasonable garden before dropping dramatically to a sandstone bed some twenty-five feet below in Smithdown Lane.

I set out along Oxford Street in search of Smithdown Lane and the tunnels, stopping to ask directions from a skinny man in his late thirties. He had a cigarette stuck to his bottom lip, and there it stayed during our brief conversation.

"Do you know the way to The Old Stable Yard?" I asked.

"Oh – lookin fo tha tunnels are ya ? Fo yehs my uncle uste to tork abowt them, an noe one ever beleeved im, bur e was ri- ght wasn' he?"

"Am I anywhere near them?"

"Depends – best way is go up past Paddy's Wigwam?"

"Pardon?"

"Yoo no – the arsie Cathedral."

"Pardon?"

"You know - the Roman Catholic Cathedral?"

"Oh, I see. The RC Cathedral – got you."

"That's right, the arsie Cathedral, keep straate on up Oxford Rode, owver Crown Streeet, an yure ther."

"Thanks."

One thing's for sure, in 21st century Liverpool, political correctness is struggling to make any impact. The Islington Brigade should spend a day or two here to see just how little impact they have actually made. The spokesperson for Liverpool Council may bang the political correctness drum, but the average Joe in the street didn't seem to give a monkey's, and I for one found it quite refreshing. There was nothing malicious in their approach, quite the reverse; there was a degree of honesty that has long since vanished in a haze of ridiculous red tape and PC jargon.

In the old stable yards on Smithdown Lane sits the entrance to the Williamson Tunnels Heritage Centre. I had a little over ten minutes to wait for the next guided tour, so I settled for a quick cup of tea in the snack bar before being introduced to a very smartly-dressed man who I took to be the boss. He was in fact Dave Roscoe, a volunteer and my guide for the next forty minutes or so. He picked up a two-way radio and a large torch, and then we both donned hard hats, before entering the 'tunnels' via a large metal door. Once inside, David proceeded to tell me the following:

"The story of the tunnels is one of conjecture, there were those who speculated that Williamson and his wife were members of a strange religious sect, and that he believed the world faced Armageddon, and the tunnels would be his salvation. I like to take a kinder view, that Joseph held genuine compassion for his fellow man. In short, he was a natural philanthropist, and his tunnels were the nineteenth century equivalent of the job creation schemes we see today."

Williamson was, it seems, far cleverer than most people gave him credit for: he had been shrewd enough to purchase a great tract of land for very little money in relative terms, the reason being that it was in the view of most people, impossible to build on. There were no mechanical means available for him to simply fill in such vast spaces, so he hit upon the idea of creating a series of arched brick ceilings and walls that simply met the level of the natural sandstone, creating a canopy for each of the voids. In some cases where the excavations were too deep for one arch, he simply built a further vaulted roof over the first arch, clearly visible in one section of the tour. So in effect, contrary to popular belief and folklore, a good deal of them weren't tunnels at all, but firm foundations for his prestigious property and gardens above.

Whatever the motives or the rationale of this unusual man, at a time when men were returning from the Napoleonic Wars with little prospect of work he certainly filled a void. By 1816 his tunnels were well and truly underway – literally. With the death of his wife in 1822, it appears Williamson became even more obsessed by his subterranian world, building living rooms and even a banqueting hall. Joseph passed away eighteen years later in 1840. We will probably never know the reasons why he built these tunnels, but built them he did. Since their discovery, tonnes of earth and collected rubbish have been removed and a good number of the tunnels are now open to the public. David Roscoe's enthusiasm and love of his topic were obvious. I won't tell you all the secrets of the tunnels because that would spoil your enjoyment, and leave David and others struggling with little to impart.

I thanked David profusely and made my way back to the city centre, but before I did, I walked up to Mason Street, to view what was essentially the front elevation of Williamson's original properties. What a mess, the whole area is now a jumble of neglected workshops and industrial activity, save for the front wall of his old house. How that has survived is nothing short of a miracle. Like all charities, the Williamson Tunnels are finding it difficult to raise the large amounts needed to continue the clearing of these unique structures. If you're ever in Liverpool take a trip up to Smithdown Lane – it's well worth a visit.

My route back into the city took me from the Anglican Cathedral – a monster of a place, designed by the architect Sir Giles Gilbert

Scott. The foundation stone was laid by Edward VII in 1904. Four monarchs and seventy-four years later (if you include Edward VIII), in October 1978, Queen Elizabeth II attended a service to mark the official completion of Britain's largest cathedral. I was maxed out on cathedrals; largest, smallest, oldest, strangest – so decided to skip the interior of this one. If you feel cheated and would like to visit this huge building, then just make your way towards the 'arsie' cathedral and you're practically in line – you can't miss it. One final twist of irony is to be found in the road that runs from Parliament Street to Oxford Street, effectively connecting the two cathedrals. Its name is Hope Street – say no more, you're in Liverpool.

Continuing on to Mount Pleasant I passed what I presumed to be the University area, based purely on the premise that I was the only guy with grey hair and not carrying a rucksack. The houses along this route were still very impressive, and though most of them either formed part of the university campus or were inhabited by businesses, it was evident that this had once been a very nice area to come home to. At the foot of the hill sat the Adelphi Hotel, an impressive white stone structure, and far larger than I remembered it. Next stop the Wallasey Tunnel and New Brighton.

Down into the bowls of the earth glides the Wallasey Tunnel. Built to relieve the traffic levels in the older Birkenhead Tunnel, the new tunnel was opened on 24th June 1971 by Queen Elizabeth II. There are in fact two tunnels set side by side. This means there is no oncoming traffic in the tunnel. This is, I think, one of the major contributors to what is a five-minute optical illusion. Once inside the tunnel the whole journey feels as though you are driving down hill, even when you reach what is effectively the base of the tunnel, because the other end is not in view and you are now in essence climbing, you still feel as though you are descending. Not until you exit the tunnel and see vehicles approaching in the opposite direction does any form of reasoning return – most odd!

I was on the other side, so to speak. With Pier Head clearly on my right across the water I headed for Wallasey Town Hall and a place to park. You get the distinct feeling that at the time this Town Hall was completed (1916 and immediately used as a military hospital), there must have been a fair degree of rivalry with their counterparts across the water. Built on a lavish scale, it is also technically back to front; in short all its grandeur faces the Mersey, in what appears to be a direct statement that 'anything Liverpool can show, we can match'. It is approached from the Mersey aspect by an impressive flight of wide steps, at the top of which sits a fourteen window-wide structure with a massive central square tower topped by an equally impressive square cupola-cum-tower (it really is a rather odd shape).

I estimated the walk along to New Brighton was no more than a mile and the day was fine and dry, so off I tootled along Seacombe Promenade. The immediate thing you notice on this side of the estuary is how much nearer to the sea you are. Whereas in Liverpool, because of the old port workings or the current usage of Pier Head, the water line is always twenty or so feet below you, here on the Seacombe Promenade there is only a shallow wall and a cast metal rail between you and the water. This is far more appealing, and you really feel as though you are at the seaside rather than simply viewing a port. Without warning, the Seacombe Promenade blends seamlessly into Egremont Promenade as it heads towards New Brighton. From this vantage point, the old Liverpool Dock buildings looked even more desolate than they had done the day before when viewed from the deck of the Mersey Ferry. It was hard to imagine that at the height of its activity, Liverpool's dock front stretched for seven miles. The majority of shipping entering Mersey water is now container-based, and heads for the thriving container terminal at Bootle. That's progress – but not very romantic, is it?

The other noticeable thing about this stretch of the promenade was how many anglers there were, and not just retired guys filling the long daylight hours. No, this was a hobby that had obviously found favour with old and young alike. All along the seawall at regular intervals, from the Town Hall to New Brighton, the folk of the Wirral Peninsula had come to chance their luck in the estuary. I stopped to chat to one local who looked more than content with his two rods anchored against the low wall.

"What do you normally catch in these waters?" I asked.

"Well, its a little early yet for the main catches, but yesterday, I caught a few codlings, give it a couple of months or so and adult cod will follow."

"So the Spanish super-trawlers haven't hoovered everything up then?"

"Not quite, and what they don't know is, the minute the adult cod arrive, the predator fish – you know, like, dogfish – will be right behind. Last October I caught no end of plump two foot long dogfish just about here."

"Two feet long, is that just a fisherman's tale?"

"No, come October this stretch of the promenade will be teaming with blokes and their tackle."

"Fancy," I replied, wished him well and strolled on.

I wasn't sure, but New Brighton was either a mirage, or the natural lay of the land was causing an optical illusion, because no matter how far I walked it didn't appear to be getting any nearer. The Egremont continued in pretty much the same vein as its predecessor for a further half mile or so. In the distance I could plainly see Fort Perch Rock, but still somehow becoming no nearer. Built between 1825 and 1829, 'The Fort' was once an integral part of Liverpool's defence system, sitting strategically at the mouth of the Mersey Estuary. At one time it was manned by up to a hundred men and armed with sixteen, 32-pounder guns, mounted on stout platforms. With defence walls that ranged in height from twenty-five foot to thirty-two foot, not for nothing was it known as the 'Gibraltar of The Mersey'. Then somehow I found myself standing at the end of Victoria Parade, Rock Point directly ahead. I think the biggest contributor to this illusion had been me. I had guessed that the distance from Seacombe to Rock Point was no more than a mile, when in reality it is nearly double that distance.

In 1830 a Liverpool merchant named James Atherton purchased a huge tract of the land at Rock Point. This position afforded great views across the Mersey and out to sea. It was also blessed with a handsome, sandy beach. Having been familiar with many of the south coast resorts, his aim was to develop an upmarket residential area for the local well-to-do, his template for such grandeur being the coastal towns of West Sussex – hence 'New Brighton'. Shortly after 1831, development began in earnest, as palatial homes began to spring up on the hillside above the estuary.

New Brighton today is clean and scrubbed, the promenade wide, impressive and traffic free. There is evidence a plenty that a genuine attempt at regeneration has been undertaken. The lovely Art Deco buildings along the sea front have been carefully restored and blend in well with the new Floral Pavilion. I wandered over to Fort Perch Rock, a stoic stone fortress now under private ownership. The notice pinned to a post at the foot of the ramp explained that the fort was now under private ownership and was undergoing a continual process of restoration – which I took to mean nothing was happening. Although the huge doors to the fort were firmly bolted, the exterior looked in good order and the seven or so flags flying high above the entrance added to the general feeling of pride in the area.

I sidled over to the nearby sea wall and, leaning on the railing, looked out over the Mersey Estuary. It wasn't, I have to admit, much of a view. Across the water my only vista for as far as the eye could see was one of low-level industrial warehousing, a mountain of shredded scrap metal, and shipping containers by the score. Not much of an outlook if you were on holiday. In fairness to New Brighton, it is a town of two halves. Stand at Perch Rock and look to your right, and your view is as previously described. Look to your left and the panorama is one of open water, a wide, handsome promenade and sandy beaches. I was joined at my viewing perch by a chap who was 'doing his hour of cycling since taking early retirement'. We chatted aimlessly about football, (he was a Liverpool supporter), politics (he was a Labour supporter) and the country in general. I won't tell you what he said about that. I asked him about New Brighton and how it was trying to claw back to its 'Glory Days'.

"When I was a youngster, we used to come down to Brighton of a weekend like, and you couldn't move. The whole of the seafront was just one mass of people, the beaches were packed and the Queens Hotel on the corner there, the one they've made into apartments, was overflowing. When it was time to go home the whole of the road from the beach to the top of the hill was lined with buses, and even then it was nothing to have to wait an hour for the next bus home. That's besides all the people who came over from the 'Pool on the ferry. Don't forget Brighton had its own terminal in those days. Have you been on the ferry yet?"

"Yes, yesterday," I replied.

"Other than at peak times they call it the Mersey Tour now don't they? I had a cousin over from Canada a couple of months ago and we took him on the ferry like. He enjoyed it, but oh that bloody tune, I couldn't get it out of my head for days."

Laughing I quipped: "Yep I know the feeling, I wonder if he gets royalties on that?" It reminded me of the time I was in Amsterdam, and decided to visit the Van Gough Museum – as soon as you step inside, and for the duration of your visit. *Vincent* by Don McLean is playing on a continual loop – that one stayed in my head for a week.

"So, what happened to New Brighton?" I asked.

"Well, look out there, where would you rather spend a week – here or on the Costa del Sol?"

"Still, its nice to spend a few hours here, on a day like today."

"Oh yeah, I cycle most days, the flat routes around here are perfect, and apart from a couple of sections where you join the main road system, I can practically reach Neston and Parkgate down the peninsula Well must get a couple more miles in before lunchtime.

All the best," and my new found friend rode off along the 'Prom'.

If New Brighton is a town of two vistas, it's also a town of two distinct types of dwellings. Viewing the rows of pretty Victorian terraced houses that rise gently from the seafront to the road above, you could be in any British seaside town, so familiar is the scene. The only difference being, if this were Morecambe, Scarborough, Hastings or the like, they would have signs in the window – ROOMS TO LET, NO VACANCIES, H&C, COL TV IN ALL ROOMS. They would carry jaunty names that bore no resemblance either geographically, or literally, to their location, names such as *Capri Villas, Belle View, Buckingham Heights* and *Dunroamin*. Here they were all private homes, not a guest house in sight, no assortment of brightly coloured façades. Instead uniform cream was the order of the day.

Walk a little further up one of the steep inclines that lead away from the hectic seafront (that last statement could have been a slight exaggeration), and you start to see James Atherton's vision in a different light. Here beautiful deluxe villas and mini-mansions sit with what would have been unencumbered views (some still have) of the estuary. This is still obviously a very pleasant place to live and, with a comfortable, traffic-free drive to the ferry at Seacombe, a mere fifteen minutes commute from central Liverpool. I was about to return to Wallasey, when in the corner of the Fort car park I spotted a sign (actually about five signs in one) and read the following:

> *This is a designated bathing beach, you are advised to swim only when a lifeguard is on duty.*
>
> *Danger: do not venture on to tidal sandbanks during incoming tide.*
>
> *When the lifeguard is on duty first aid facilities are available at Victoria Road lookout.*

Warning: do not swim anywhere on the Wirral coast-line if the red flag is flying.

The designated personal watercraft launch site at Victoria Road South New Brighton – a vehicle permit is required.

Is it me, or do these councils have a designated bod whose sole edict is to bark instructions at people? How about a sign that tells you what you can do – a sort of happy notice board for visitors:

You can eat as much ice cream as you like.

Also huge quantities of burgers and chips.

The fresh air is free, so take as much as you like.

Park for nothing (actually the parking is free in New Brighton, but they don't make a big deal of it).

Smile while you are here and someone will always smile back.

There we are, isn't that so much nicer ? Not a penny extra on the rates and the local ice cream man is delighted – it's a win-win situation.

My friend on the bike had struck a chord when he'd mentioned Neston. An immeasurable amount of time had passed since I last visited the Dee Estuary and as I was practically on top of the place, this seemed as good a time as any to re-visit. The drive from New Brighton was speedy due to the close proximity of the M53 motorway, and within less than twenty minutes I was following the signs for Clatterbridge (I wonder where that name comes from).

I proceeded at a stately pace towards Neston; that was, until I drove into Thornton Hough. What a beauty. This picture-postcard village was the last thing I'd expected to see, but so arresting was the place that I simply parked up and grabbed my camera for what I knew could only be great snaps. From the simply stunning St George's Church, complete with the most glorious gated entrance to the black and white cottages and smithy, this little village was almost too perfect. It had all the hallmarks of a place that had not so much evolved over the centuries, but had been laid out by a benevolent architect.

I wasn't far off the mark. At the end of the 18th century, Thornton Hough formed part of the Neston Estate owned by Baron Mostyn. Sounds rather threatening, doesn't it? The population was a mere 165 in 1801, when Joseph Hirst took ownership of a good percentage of the village. Joseph built a church and the first school in Thornton Hough. By 1880 Lord Leverhulme (of Lever Bros, soap manufacturers) had moved into the area and set about acquiring and rebuilding property, principally for the benefit of his estate workers. The whole layout is very reminiscent of the style he later employed at Port Sunlight: spacious village greens, chocolate-box-pretty houses and a wealth of amenities including tennis courts, cricket pitch and a village hall. There must have been far worse places to live in the 1890s. With Thornton Hough suitably recorded for posterity, I pressed on to Neston and Parkgate.

I passed through Neston, very pretty but nothing so startling as to require noting – sorry Neston – instead I turned due right for Parkgate. I parked the car on the main street and ventured forth into Parkgate. In truth, there isn't a lot to venture into. Sitting on the Dee Estuary, this sleepy little village was once an important embarkation point for Ireland. The Dee at the beginning of the 18th century came to within fifty yards of the main street. Over the years the Dee silted up alarmingly, until it was impossible to use Parkgate as a port. Looking out over a mile or more of Marshland to the estuary, it is hard to believe that anything larger than a rowing boat managed to sail into Parkgate.

Below the wall level a man in a high-vis jacket, carrying a bin-liner and one of those sticks fitted with a grab claw, was busy clearing the first ten yards or so of the marshland. Stopping to talk to him (this had been a very chatty day all in all), I asked him how far he reckoned the marshes stretched.

"At least a mile, maybe a mile and a quarter, you can walk across to the other side when the tide's out, if you're careful."

"Have you ever done it?" I asked.

"No, don't trust it. It was bad enough what happened about two years ago. I'd been working this stretch for about three years, and never once seen the tide come within more than a quarter mile or so of the wall. I must have been about a hundred yards out and busy clearing stuff, when I suddenly felt something by my feet – I turned round and a high tide had come right in. Within another five minutes I would have been cut off completely as the tide was lapping the wall."

I looked at the huge expanse of marshland between us and the Dee.

"I don't think there's much chance of that today."

"No, I think I'm fairly safe for now."

I said cheerio to the man with the stick and walked off to delve a little deeper into the history of Parkgate.

Among the luminaries this area can lay claim to one of the most notorious (and a regular visitor to Parkgate in her later years) was Emy Lyon, later Emma Hart, but known to you and me as Lady Hamilton, she of Lord Nelson fame. Born in the nearby village of Ness in 1761, she was known in later life to swim here ('most beneficial for her skin complaint' – don't ask). The composer Handel and the preacher John Wesley are known to have sailed from here, although there is no documentation to suggest that it was on the same ship. Our old friend Baron Mostyn's influence is still felt here, in the guise of a black and white fronted junior and senior school that stretches unendingly along the high street and boasts a large sign that clearly states – Mostyn House School. The whole of the front line of Parkgate is easy on the eye and obviously a very popular place for locals. Speaking of which, I had spotted a huge suspension bridge across the estuary some four or so miles in the distance and stopped a lady to ask what it was called – it obviously linked the mainland to Wales, because even I had worked out that those were the Welsh Hills in the distance. Even now I'm still struggling to come to terms with her reply.

"Oh! I'm sorry, I don't know. I'm local but I've never noticed it before."

What? Somebody builds a sodding great suspension bridge with a centre stanchion that rises God knows how many hundred feet in the air, with tons of wire cables suspended in majestic swoops… and you never even noticed it? What the hell do they put in the water around here? She must have been out of her skull for the past five years or so. Ironically, I spotted the same lady leaving the newsagents, engrossed in her daily paper – it's important to keep up with what's going on, isn't it?

What Did The Romans Do For Us?

Chester – or to use its original name Deva – started out as a fort around AD74-77, as far as anyone can accurately date. Emperor Claudius (AD41-54) had ordered the invasion of Britain in AD43 and the location at the River Dee was strategically useful, as there were plans to sail from the Dee to invade nearby Ireland and North Wales. Around this time, Deva was considered to be almost as important as Londinium (London). By the time the time Deva – a Celtic word meaning 'goddess of the waters' – was settled, Rome had a new Emperor: Vespasian (AD69-79), a military leader whose building programme and foresight contributed greatly to the stability of ancient Britain.

The Romans stayed for another four hundred years or so, during which time they established a road system, built villas and towns, installed drains, under-floor heating, created a system of governance and, much to the chagrin of the Welsh, introduced the leek. Evidence of their tenure in Chester is everywhere, from the amphitheatre to the Roman walls and bridges.

With little alternative but to park in the NCP car park (always so affordable aren't they?), I strolled the short distance to central Chester. The nicest part about this historic city is that once you've crossed the manic ring road – they really are busy – you find yourself in a peaceful traffic-free time-warp, where beautiful black and white buildings with raised walkways lead tantalisingly to its heart. These are the Rows. The original layout dates back as far as the 14th century. Towards the end of the 15th century, householders began a process of gradually enlarging their properties. This was principally done by extending the chamber over the single-story Row and supporting it on posts. The gap between these posts and the street walkway was then covered, thus extending the stallboard. Gradually the street-level shop gained an additional shop front above, and these became the basis for the Rows we see today – a sort of Tudor shopping mall.

Towards the end of the Victorian era, Chester started to realise the value of its existing Rows, both architecturally and fiscally. Instead of the commonly-held views of the previous century – unpopular, unfashionable and dirty – they were now being acclaimed as unique and picturesque. They were also doing no harm to the tourist trade. A team of local architects led by Thomas Mainwaring Penson, and including Thomas Meakin Lockwood, John Douglas with several other interested parties laid plans to restore or, where necessary, completely rebuild in the black and white Tudor style we see today. The Rows were retained and improved with one exception: Shoemakers' Row near Northgate Street, but this was sadly redeveloped towards the end of the 19th century.

Like everyone else who visits Chester, I automatically gravitated toward the upper Rows. They really are charming, with their uneven boarded floors, decorative balcony rails and low ceilings. The shops, although governed by the width of the front entrance space, appeared positively cavernous in their depth, and as for some of the goods on display, if I ever take up smoking the pipe, I know where to come for a quality Meerschaum. The other trick that Chester has pulled off with a great deal of aplomb is their indoor shopping centre. Where most towns and cities have in the past simply bulldozed acres of fine buildings in their rush for concrete and steel, the planners at Chester Council obviously sat down and, against all perceived wisdom, thought about their idea in depth. The result is the Grosvenor Centre – a modern, airy precinct with a good size multi-storey car park that nobody can spot from the outside. You simply wander in and out via the Rows, and how much more pleasant it is for that. Nothing assaults the senses, and Chester has the best of both worlds – modern shops dressed in black and white splendour. Perfect !

It really was a joy to move around this city, and for the next hour or so I walked the Rows without a care. Up and down odd angled staircases and uneven floors I sauntered happily, and by default rather than design found myself by a set of steep steps that led to the city walls. From this high vantage point it was easy to see the protection these defences would have offered in times past. There would be little chance of marauding Celts creeping up unnoticed while any reasonable sentry was on duty.

Walking only one station back towards the River Dee, I descended the steps to Pepper Street and the amphitheatre. The sun was warming and the sky filled with puff ball white clouds as I made my way towards this major archaeological site. Set in a very central area of Chester, this is Britain's largest known amphitheatre. It was used by the Romans for both entertainment and military training for the 20th Legion. It is difficult to imagine the actual size this would have been during its time of use. The wide sweeping walls, now clearly visible, are just the edge of the original arena, and the stepped seating area would have taken up almost as much again. Circumscribed by a one-way traffic route, the arena appears smaller than it obviously was. The central area of the theatre is temporarily sand-filled to protect it until the next archaeological dig, although it's still possible to walk on and view the amphitheatre from a gladiator's perspective. There is a viewing platform, but any contemplative silence is drowned out by the passing traffic. What you can deduce, however, is that it had a pretty impressive North Procession entrance. This was one of at least two huge archways which are believed to have led into the arena. My favourite part of this archaeological site however, was the shrine to Nemesis – the Goddess of Fate and Divine Vengeance. Here the gladiators would stop and offer prayers to their goddess, prior to hacking each other to pieces for the benefit of the watching Consul. There are plans afoot by English Heritage and the local council to open up the whole space of the amphitheatre, as opposed to the half-circle that currently exists, but progress seems rather slow at the moment. If I were to gamble on these aspirations coming to fruition – I'd have said the odds were about 50–1.

In fairness to the local council and other preservation bodies in Chester, they have a major task in hand. Most towns, and even some cities, have less than a handful of historical monuments and sites to look after – Chester is stuffed with them from end to end. How you define just what is a priority must be nigh impossible. On the other hand my immediate priority was food, so I ambled back into the city for some scoff.

Those of you who have followed my previous writing will know I am a bit of a coffee lover. I like to think I'm not addicted, but wherever I find myself, I am drawn to the blue sign of Caffé Nero. This is not to say that other establishments don't serve equally tasty beverages, it's just for me Nero hits the spot – on reflection, quite appropriate in a Roman city. So it was without much persuasion that I found myself sitting in their Chester branch, contentedly sipping on my cappuccino and taking man-sized bites out of a BLT panini, which is more than can be said for the chap sat adjacent to me. From the corner of my eye I watched as he surgically attended to a pain au raisin. I was familiar with this style of eating. My teenage son Edward can remove the whole chocolate covering from a choc ice before eventually devouring the ice cream – which to me rather defeats the object of eating a choc ice in the first place. I liken this style of picky eating to a rodent; the similarity to a rat or a squirrel is quite striking when observed by a third party. This particular guy's actions seemed even more fascinating, as he was in possession of a rather sharp nose and slightly protruding ears. In fact, he was appearing more rodent-like by the minute. I can speak from some experience when it comes to the pain au raisin because this is normally my pastry of choice to accompany a morning coffee. For me this is a treat that can be finished off in approximately four manly bites, five at a pinch. Roland Rat was now systematically picking out the raisins, with all the skill of a surgeon. Once the pain au raisin was simply a pain, he then started unwinding the circular pastry and breaking off tiny pieces. I had finished my panini and was seriously tempted to amble over, nick his pastry, and gobble it in one. It's truly amazing how interesting people can be when you're not pressed for time. Or conversely this could be a severe case of too much lateral thinking and strong coffee.

Chester is a city of constant distractions and surprises. You're ambling along minding your own business, when you turn a corner and are faced with another tempting vista. I don't think I've ever been anywhere where there is so much history packed into what is essentially a compact area. The original grid system for the streets of Chester was laid down by the Romans and is still recognizable today, added to which the city walls obviously helped to prevent the wholesale development witnessed in so many other major cities in the UK. These distractions come in many forms: an intriguing alleyway, a near-vertical set of stone steps – leading who knew where, and in this case a whopping red sandstone cathedral, shoe-horned into a cobbled square. The setting is really rather incongruous for such grandeur. It's rather like viewing an outsized piece placed in what is otherwise a perfect scale model. I have a vague recollection of visiting Chester Cathedral on some form of junior school trip. I also have hazy schoolboy memories of this being a monastery before its conversion to an Anglican Cathedral. I was about to find out whether my boyhood memories were anywhere near the mark.

Records show that as early as 660 AD a church existed here and in 875 the relics of St Werburgh were brought to Chester to protect them from attacks by the Vikings (that would do the trick). In 907 a church was built by King Alfred's daughter, Queen Ethelfelda ('the Lady of The Mercians'), specifically to house remains of St Werburgh. The bones might have worked for the Vikings, but they had little effect against the Normans because, by 1092, the Earl of Chester was a Norman by the name of Hugh Lupus ('the Wolf'), nephew of William the Conqueror. Hugh decided to establish a great monastery in the heart of his administrative capital. He sought the help of Abbot Anselm of Bec in Normandy, one of the greatest theologians of his day. Anselm, after much persuading, came to Chester to oversee the new foundation. Construction of the monastery began in 1092. I was right, my dusty memory bank was not playing tricks on me.

Wow! This is a whopper. The surroundings may be compact and the approach sudden, rather than impressive and expected, but once inside this is a building built to impress. The size of the building was only matched by the admission fee – £5. I don't want to get all uppity, but there is still something that doesn't chime with me and church entrance fees. Whether it's the Money Men in the Temple syndrome, I'm not sure, but there wasn't going to be an option, so I prized a blue note from my padlocked wallet and strode into the Cathedral. The Cathedral is simply stunning. A huge vaulted nave rises to 78 feet and spans a staggering 75 feet, leading to a central tower (an awe inspiring 127 feet), choir stalls, the altar and Lady Chapel, the whole dissected by a north and south transept. I read the usual wall plaques and memorial stones dotted along the side wall of the knave until I came to the south transept, where a very impressive tomb is topped by a white marble figure at rest. This is the burial place of Hugh Lupus Grosvenor, Duke of Westminster KG, 1825–1899. Lupus, where had I heard that name before? Of course, the Wolf, William's nephew.

At each of the four main extremities was a stained-glass window. With the added bonus of a sunny day, they were nothing short of breathtaking in their beauty and craftsmanship. I moved across to the north transept and an ancient doorway that leads to the Chapter House and the cloisters. This section of the building dates back to 1200 AD and between the Norman pillars six of the 13th century abbots are at rest. The cloisters are of a later date –1526, and open out onto a secluded garden. When originally in use as an abbey, the only source of warmth came via a large solitary fire place (this really was for brass monk-ese). I crossed the central floor once more, and headed for the 13th century Lady Chapel and the stone shrine of St Werburgh which dates from the 14th century and is used to contain her relics. The shrine, made from the same pink stone as the cathedral, has a pierced base and the upper section in the form of a miniature chapel, contained several statuettes. During the dissolution of the monasteries it was dismantled. Some of the parts were found during the 1873 restoration of the cathedral and the shrine was reassembled in 1888 – very nice too. I think I'd had my fiver's worth and the warm sunshine was beckoning.

Blinking alarmingly as I returned to modern-day Chester, I studied my mini guide. Back to the walls I think! Ascending the steps by the ring road, I was walking high over Chester. Or at least I was for two hundred yards or so, when I came to a full stop against a solid gate with a notice explaining that this small section of the wall was closed for essential repairs – I don't know, can't these Romans build anything to last? Following the diversion sign I crossed the far end of a car park and the Grosvenor shopping centre before exiting under the Clock Tower on Eastgate Street. Here I rejoined the City Walls, passing directly under the famous Clock Tower. The clock was built to commemorate the diamond jubilee of Queen Victoria in 1897. As usual nothing could be done without the forming of a committee to oversee such an illustrious monument (not a lot changes, does it?). They agreed that a subscription fund should be opened and donors would have a chance to subscribe for one of three selected causes – the Jubilee Institute of Nurses, a memorial tower and clock on Eastgate, or festivities and public rejoicings (I'd have gone for the last one). Although the clock was initially an outside bet, the other two causes being more popular, the chimes won the day and by December 1897 the process of erecting a decorative clock had begun. The result is a wonderfully ornate, wrought-iron cased clock in high Victorian style, complete with a verdigris domed top and ornate finials. Outside of London (Big Ben), this is probably the most photographed clock in the UK.

If you want to get a true perspective on Chester, past and present, it is essential to walk the City Walls. The normally hidden views you encounter on undertaking this hike are rewarding in the extreme. For instance, having originally approached the cathedral from ground level, I had no idea how perfect the rear setting to this building is. Surrounded by lush green lawns and peppered with sumptuous trees and shrubs, it is sublime. The route in turn leads to Deanery Fields, part of the cathedral precinct. Beneath the grass are the remains of the Roman barracks and fortress, said to have housed in excess of 5,500 troops from various locations across the Empire.

The first major point of interest along the Walls is the King Charles Tower – it is recorded that from here, on Sept 24th 1645, King Charles watched as his army were defeated by parliamentary forces on Rowton Moor. It is more likely that what he actually witnessed was the scattered and disparate remnant of his forces, as they were pursued towards Chester. Whatever the history, this is certainly a great vantage point – to my right, the wall dropped dramatically away to the Shropshire Union Canal far below, while to the left the hills of Wales were clearly visible.

As I approached Northgate I came across two small houses set at wall level. The last thing I had expected to see whilst walking the City Walls was a bookshop, but that is exactly what I did stumble upon. The Bluecoat Bookshop is run by two charming ladies named Kath and Jane. Within a single room are packed more new books than anyone could conceive possible. Obviously a great deal of their trade was carried out via their website, as the front desk was piled high with Jiffy bags ready for posting. The subject matter on display was very impressive and there seemed barely an interest that wasn't catered for. They were chatty and helpful, and I highly recommend a visit next time you are in Chester. Their address is also equally memorable – No 1 City Walls, Chester.

Without warning the Walls suddenly stop at a concrete bridge that spans the busy by-pass. I suppose it's better than allowing roaring traffic through the centre of this historic city, but it comes as something of a shock to be vaulted from a peaceful Roman walkway into a 21st century mêlée. Once safely over the bridge, the City Walls returns to its tranquil origins.

I stopped to read the inscription above Pemberton's Parlour. Here the wall and accompanying hand rail bows out in a sweeping semi-circle. Leaning against the rail, both myself and a friendly Irish man from Dublin, tried to decipher the faded wording on the plaque above the recess. The chap had come over from Ireland for the wedding of his niece in Shrewsbury and proceeded to tell me in a wonderful lilting accent:

"All my life I've read about Chester, but never managed to make the trip, so there we are attending this lovely wedding in Shrewsbury, and even the weather stayed fine, and you can't always rely on that can you? Where was I? Oh yes, Shrewsbury... so I said to the wife, 'how do you fancy another week in Chester?' Well she smiles and says 'yes', and here we are."

I didn't know whether I dared ask another question for fear of not getting home before dark.

Eventually, we deciphered the stone tablet. Roughly translated it read – 'Once known as Dille's Tower, then the Goblin Tower, it was rebuilt in the 18th century as part of improvements to the Walls. The present name is attributed to John Pemberton, a local business man who made ropes in the area below the wall and used the tower to keep an eye on his workmen.'

A model employer keen to keep an eye on their welfare no doubt.

I said goodbye to my Irish friend, but not before he had left me with a parting thought.

Having noticed my camera, he said "I'll tell you, you can't take a bad shot in Chester if you tried."

On reflection I think he is probably correct.

The wall continues for some way before coming to an abrupt end at the semi-derelict Bonewaldesthorne's Tower. Here a spur forks left and from this point onwards, the Walls are less complete until picked up once again nearer the River Dee. I passed the Old Infirmary, now (judging by the vehicles parked outside) converted into luxury apartments. With the Infirmary on one side and the ancient Queen's School on the other, I made my way back towards Bridge Street. As I walked past what was obviously the kitchen of the Queen's School, my nostrils were assaulted by a cooking smell so familiar, it instantly transported me back to my junior school days. This wasn't the modern-day school cuisine of burgers and fries, but the mash potato, woody carrots and cabbage of my childhood. I felt at once a mixture of nostalgia and revulsion – never has a smell stirred such vivid memories and emotions.

Returning to the old cross at the junction of Eastgate and Bridge Street, my spirits lifted to new heights. The sun was out, the day was fine, and as if by order, there was a young musician sat playing by the base of the cross. Instead of some of the less gifted performers you come across in these situations, this boy was talented. With no amplification in sight, he played his acoustic guitar to perfection, and the tune Cavotina was just perfect. I decided there and then, that if there is a God, he was in Chester that day.

I rejoined the Rows in Bridge Street. Despite the crowded shopping areas and the general feeling of wellbeing in Chester, this city had not escaped unscathed from the recent worldwide recession. I counted at least ten empty shops along this covered walkway. As little as two years ago, you would have had to kill someone to get your hands on one of these retail spaces. Now you had the pick of ten. On crossing Grosvenor Street, Bridge St becomes Lower Bridge St, and as the name changes, so does the property. You leave behind the black and white medieval buildings and enter a street of Georgian splendour. Grand houses and elegant terraced rows such as Bridge Place lead gently down to the River Dee.

The afternoon was hot. I know, UK… summer… hot… not exactly words we normally use in the same sentence, but it really was very pleasant as I walked by the side of the Dee. In the distance I could see the lines of rowing boats bobbing in the gentle swell as families zig-zagged the river in those wonderful put-put motorboats. You know the sort, where you flatten the accelerator and push the craft up to a screaming three miles per hour. My intended mode of transport was a little larger, although whether it would be any faster remained to be seen. I was heading for the *Mark Twain* river cruiser. Of all the names you could have called a river cruiser on the Dee, I'd have thought Mark Twain was the last one. I had no knowledge that the man himself had ever visited Chester – that's not to say that he didn't; he had popped up in some odd places in his lifetime. I simply didn't get the connection.

This craft didn't resemble a Mississippi Steamer. There was no paddle wheel, just a lazy, bubbling, diesel engine. Surely a more appropriate name would have been *The Cestrian* or *The Rampant Duke*, at the very least *The City of Chester*, but no – *Mark Twain* was my river transport for the next forty minutes or so.

The River Dee is extremely wide. Not Mississippi-wide but very beamy none-the-less. Once away from the landing stage and into the centre of the river, the whole view of Chester takes on a completely different tone. Gone is the black and white picture-postcard view, replaced by impressive riverside mansion houses and, a short distance from the city centre, the stunning Deva terrace, a row of fourteen three -storey Victorian houses built in a Georgian style. This was the sort of place where you would be happy to sit in a relaxing lounger and watch all those tourists go past on the *Mark Twain*, and leisurely think to yourself – why Mark Twain? The sun, now piercing through the windows of the boat, was burning my right ear – that's right, burning my ear. I shuffled along the seat to avoid the rays, but to no avail – a red ear it would have to be. I tell you, I suffer for my craft. One day nearly frozen on the Yorkshire Moors – the next, suffering sunstroke on the Dee. Red ear apart, this was very pleasant. Not exciting, just pleasant.

In just over fifteen minutes we turned across the river and started our return journey. Almost as soon as we had completed this manoeuvre, the tannoy crackled into life. Unfortunately, a lot of the commentary was drowned out by the thumping of the diesel engines, so what I heard was odd snatched phrases and sentences between the engine revs. The result being something like:

"On the right-hand side you will see the riverside house boats and cot… some of them worth… but totally uninsurable because of the high… a little further along we see the Famous King's School rowing… and their many craft all… Now we are passing the very fine Chester Rowing Club and their wonderful riverside… and boathouse."

This intermittent commentary continued for the whole of the return journey and, apart from one section by Broughton, when for some reason the engines pulled back, the information was delivered in code. The one audible part of the demented information I did pick up though, was pure gold, and something I think I would have so easily missed had it not been for this trip. Overlooking the river at Broughton sits an impressive red brick church. Follow the line of the church down to the river and in between is Gallows Hill. Now known as Barrel Well Hill (more anon), this is now consecrated ground, so no building will ever take place on this prime piece of land. This was the place where so many were brought to meet their gruesome end. Witches and non-believers, petty criminals, murderers and, sadly, the insane, all took their last gasp view of the River

Dee from this spot. Though by far the most bizarre form of trial and punishment came via the act that now gives its name to the area – Barrel Well Hill. The process was used as a test of truth for determining whether some poor soul was, or wasn't, a witch. The defendant was placed in a barrel at the top of the hill, then ceremoniously let loose to roll down the hill and into the Dee. If the unfortunate woman (it was predominantly women) died in the process, this was proof of her innocence and her soul would be received by Christ as a true Christian innocent. However, if she escaped from the barrel, she was deemed to be guilty, pulled out of the Dee, then taken away to be hung. How fair is that? In racing terms that's not even an each way bet. This would certainly put you off owning a black cat or wearing an unusual piece of headgear.

I left *Mark Twain* with the smell of diesel in my nostrils, the sound of the throbbing engine buzzing in my head and one bright red ear. All in all though, I enjoyed the trip. Purchasing an ice cool bottle of fresh orange from a riverside kiosk, I sat on a wall near Bridgegate and watched the hypnotic overflow of the weir. The weir was constructed not, as first thought, by the Romans but by the Normans in 1092. They created a head of water that made the area around the Dee Bridge, Chester's powerhouse from that time on. Mills developed just west of the bridge to grind corn into flour, vital for the growing population of Chester. In medieval times they also generated a sizeable income for the Earl of Chester and later the Crown, via a levy called a 'multure'. Water-powered mills also sprung up on the Handbridge side of the weir. The last mill built on this site was a tobacco factory, which sadly closed in 1954, and was subsequently demolished in the 1960s to make way for the residential properties – Salmon Leap. The weir and the Dee today look tranquil and positively inert when compared to their original industrial useage, but don't be fooled by appearances. The River Dee is still the main source of water supply for the inhabitants of Chester, and further fills Thomas Telford's famed Shropshire Union Canal.

Blimey this sun's hot!

Leaving the riverside in the direction of the Roman Gardens, I came upon a centurion in full dress complete with helmet, sword and leather sandals. This wasn't a spectre of ancient Chester, but a 21st century man, dressed for the much praised 'Roman Tour'. Surrounded by approximately twenty junior centurions, all sporting grey plastic body armour, he was explaining that the wall at this point, where it met the embankment, was twenty-five feet tall. He then posed the question to the awestruck eight year olds:

"How tall do you think this wall was in Roman times?"

There was a moment's silence, broken by one little chap who blurted out, "Six feet high".

"No, sorry, it was in fact, twice this height when Chester was a Roman Fort."

What? Fifty feet tall? Surely not, I thought, refraining from joining in the conversation. Even on a simple mathematical scale the base of the wall would have to be twice as thick as it is now to avoid simply toppling over, but hey, what do I know? I'm not a centurion.

I had one last place to visit before I departed the rows and walls of Chester – the Roodee. No more than a five-minute stroll from the centre of Chester sits one of the country's oldest racecourses. Horse racing was believed to have started in this spot as early as 1540 (and to quote the old joke - my horse still hasn't come in yet). Still in use for major races and a variety of public events, the setting is just perfect. Once a salt marsh in Roman times, it was converted to meadowland in the middle ages as the Dee continued to silt up, extending the area to its present size. The name Roodee is derived from 'Rood' for cross and 'Eye' for island or meadow. Above the racecourse on a high promontory sits Curzon Park, developed in the 1840s as an exclusive suburb to attract Liverpool's wealthy merchants. For once, the Scousers were pipped to the post. The villas proved so popular that they needed little marketing to Liverpool's elite and were instead snapped up by local wealthy families, principal amongst which were my namesake 'The Browns', owners of the upmarket department store on Eastgate.

It was time to move on, back to the car park and replenish the coffers of NCP. How much? I asked the very pleasant man in the kiosk, as I passed him my debit card (I'd run out of cash).

"Eight pounds, sir," was his reply.

"Eight pounds," I repeated – several times, I think.

Obviously used to people in deep shock (he probably had a bottle of smelling salts in his booth, such was his calm and charming manner), he gently prized the card from my tight grip, ran it through the machine and lifted the barrier.

"There we are, sir, enjoy your day."

I bloody well was doing until five minutes ago.

If you lived within the city boundaries of Chester and wanted to borrow a reasonable sum of money, who would you ask? A good place to start, maybe, would be a man who owns a large slice of Belgravia, London; property in Grosvenor Square; numerous shopping centres and industrial estates; has immense personal wealth; is related to royalty; and owns an 11,500 acre estate just outside Chester.

We are talking of course about Major-General Gerald Cavendish Grosvenor – the sixth Duke of Westminster, KG, CB, OBE, TD and DL – try putting that on an SAE. Gerald left Harrow with a single O Level, then alarmingly failed the entrance examination for the Royal Military Academy Sandhurst. In 1970 he joined the Territorial Army as a trooper. So far so, er, good. Within three years he had slid under the radar at Sandhurst and went on to command the Cheshire Yeomanry Squadron, the North Irish Horse, and the Queen's Own Yeomanry – isn't it fantastic how far you can progress with one O Level? The Duke was at one time the country's wealthiest man with an estimated fortune of £7 billion ($14 billion). This title was lost to the owner of Chelsea Football Club, Roman Abramovich (although he's Russian, so I don't know if that counts?). Most of his wealth is derived from property in central London, where he owns approximately three hundred acres of the most exclusive commercial and residential property in Mayfair and Belgravia (including the land on which the US Embassy stands, in Grosvenor Square). In addition, he has estates in Lancashire, Cheshire and Scotland. What would he own if he'd achieved a couple of A Levels?

A mere five-minute drive from the centre of Chester in the direction of Wrexham sits the entrance to Eaton Hall, the ancestral home of the Grosvenor family. When writing a travelogue such as this you can get to the stage where the thought of another stately home can turn from pleasure to dread. So it came as a welcome surprise to find out that this was not just another Neo-Classical pile (wonderful though they are) but a pink, birthday-cake chateau.

The Grosvenor family have resided at Eaton Estate since the 1440s. Unlike most stately homes, where there have been additions and minor modifications over the centuries, but the building has kept some semblance of continuity. The Grosvenor family appear to have been somewhat more radical in their approach to construction and preservation. Over the years Eaton Hall has been rebuilt several times almost, it seems, on a whim, to match the architectural fashions of the day. Around the late 17th century, the original hall was replaced with a grand house, designed by William Sanwell. This building lasted a short time in historical terms when, on the death of the first Earl Grosvenor in 1802, he was succeeded by his son, who, between 1804 and 1812, set about the creation of a large Gothic-Georgian Mansion (an odd mix of styles even for that period). By the time the third Earl (later the first Duke of Westminster) inherited Eaton in 1869 this style of house was deeply unfashionable. So guess what? That's right. In came the demolition men. The Duke's very comfortable income meant that the New Hall, completed in 1881, cost today's equivalent of £35m to build.

This was the age of vast house parties, principally made popular by Edward, Prince of Wales, where guests were entertained on a scale unimaginable today. With parkland for the house extending to a thousand acres, and fifty acres of formal gardens and terraces, you could say this was a rather impressive house. The Victorian-Gothic style of the house was created by our old friend Alfred Waterhouse (of Manchester Town Hall fame), and was meticulously executed in every detail. This was a huge house by any standard, consisting of one hundred and fifty bedrooms, a huge stable block, kennels and a private chapel with a tower that soared to 183 feet. During the Second World War the house was used as a hospital, then a Naval College. Following hostilities, it was let on a long-term lease to the Army, who used it as an Officer Cadet Training School, until they too departed in the late 1950s. The trustees of the current Duke - due to his young age - decided that the house was too costly to maintain, and so once again Eaton Hall was torn down, in the year 1961 (where were English Heritage on that day I wonder?). The only parts to escape the bulldozer were the stable blocks and the chapel. Six years elapsed before a new, much smaller property was built. This proved to be an unpopular move all round so, in the 1990s, the present Duke remodelled the house basing it on a Classical French Chateau.

So here we leave the present Duke and his family and their unusual 'Pink Chateau'. I presume, based on family history, it will only be a matter of time before the next generation of Grosvenors replace this pastiche with a 21st century Glass House or some other oddity.

Taking The Waters

I love train journeys, and in the days before our wonderful privatisa-tion (thank you John Major) you could board the 10.50am train from Manchester Piccadilly to London Euston and, once past Stoke-on-Trent, you could vacate your second-class seat and sit in the dining car. If you ate very slowly your meal would last almost until London. Everybody knew what was going on, but nobody cared; you were buying a meal so were entitled to stay in the dining car. The carriage was full and everybody was happy. Then some bright spark decided that the on-board dining facilities should be restricted to first-class passengers only. So at the stroke of a pen, class segrega-tion was reintroduced.

I am explaining this as background to one particular journey and a wonderful lunch companion I encountered. The train had just passed through Stoke-on-Trent when I made my way to the dining car and took my seat for lunch. The carriage was rather quiet this day and before long I was passing pleasantries with an elderly gentleman who invited me to join him. No sooner had I sat down than the old boy ordered a half bottle of champagne (yes you could get champagne in the dining car then – I wouldn't know about now, because I can't afford a first-class ticket). This rapidly vanished and he ordered a repeat bottle, followed in due course by a third. It turned out that my travelling companion had shares in several hotels, one in Bournemouth, another in Torquay and more unusually one in Buxton, Derbyshire, where he had spent the last three days. He was, he told me, 'on the verge of selling his share in this Peak District Hotel. I love the place dearly but it's too far away from my home in London and it's the most difficult to promote'. Eventually, after what seemed a mere half hour or so, but was in fact over two hours, the train rolled into Euston Station and I said goodbye to this gentleman, and in a slightly squiffy state, proceeded to negotiate the long platform. This experience and conversation had stuck in the back of my mind for the best part of two decades, but was brought clearly back into focus as I stood outside the very building he had spoken of, the St Anne's Hotel on the Crescent in Buxton.

The Cavendish Family built this stunning Georgian crescent and above it the handsome façade of the Family's twin stag coat of arms, carved in stone, is still clearly visible. This and several other prominent buildings go to make up what is known locally as new Buxton. The older, original Buxton sits at the top of a steep gradient, and this is where I headed off to first.

At the crest of the hill that leads from central Buxton sits a delightful market square with period-looking shops and an impressive Town Hall. Directly in front of the Town Hall sits the Market Cross, and perched on the second and third steps of the cross was the biggest wolfhound I've ever seen – he was simply enormous. I stopped to talk to his owner, a small, stout lady who was waiting for her husband to return.

"My goodness, that's some dog. Will he grow any bigger than his current size? How old is he?" I asked.

"No he won't grow much now, he's three years old, he will just fill out like his older brother."

"You've got two of them, what does it cost to feed them?"

"Too much!" she exclaimed. "We feed them on birds."

"Pardon?"

"Not flying birds! It's the name of the select food we buy for them."

"He must certainly take some feeding all the same?"

"Yes I suppose he does, but he's as soft as a brush, very placid, apart from when he sees a cat, then he just goes mad. He can't stand them."

I wished them both well but refrained from patting or stroking him, and thanked my lucky stars that I had no feline tendencies.

At the end of Market Square is Bath Road, and a short distance along this pleasant thoroughfare sits the Church of St Ann. I think this has to be one of the smallest functioning churches I've ever seen; it's certainly very old and very unusual. The Chapel of St Anne became a place of thanksgiving during a time when Buxton was famous for its Holy Wells (believed to have unique healing properties). The activities of some of the congregation during these celebrations, where people would hang up their crutches in the church as a token of their commitment to what was viewed by Cromwell's followers as 'pagan practices', led to the eventual closure of the chapel. Following the closure, a new church was built in 1625, and dedicated to St John the Evangelist. The little church was, over the next couple of centuries, used as a school, then briefly as a mortuary chapel, before lying abandoned until 1885, when it was restored and rededicated to St Anne. Inside is a Saxon font, found nearby and returned to its rightful place within the church in 1905. It really is a most delightful little place and well worth a peek next time you are in Buxton.

Also worth a peek, and no more than a couple of strides away from the church, is Scrivener's Bookshop. This place has to be seen to be believed. Here spread over five floors is a veritable feast for any book lover. With over 40,000 second-hand books on display, it specializes in antiquarian, out-of-print literary oddities, and is owned by Alexander Scrivener who originally started the business as a book binders. I spoke to Gill, one of three ladies who help Alexander with his rather quirky business. She told me that 'it had always been a shop and that Alexander had never intended to use the property as a bookshop, but after moving in, he realised it was far too big for bookbinding alone. So he decided to stock a few books. The books like Topsy, sort of grew and grew'. You can say that again, it is cram-jammed full of every subject imaginable, from leather-bound classic fiction, art, topography, travel and music, to 1970s sci-fi. And as part of Scrivener's blurb proudly announces –

> *There are seats around the shop, free drink-making facilities, and on the second floor, a loo and a harmonium.*

What the significance of those two items in advertising terms is, I have no idea, but it certainly raises the benchmark for Waterstone's. After the obligatory wander around this wonderful emporium and complete time warp, taking in the mini museum and the harmonium, I thanked Gill and her colleagues, and returned to the 21st century.

Well that was the intention, until half way down the main street I spotted the Buxton Museum & Art Gallery. What a rare treat this turned out to be. Built in 1880 at the peak of Buxton's fame as a Spa Town, it was originally the Peak Hydropathic Hotel. Entrance is via a wide door that sits diagonally to the street, and once inside there are still enough original features left to affirm that this was once a very commodious hotel. The staircase and Art Nouveau, stained-glass panels reinforced this grand structure.

There was little to commend the downstairs exhibits, and I was about to leave (at least I hadn't had to pay any admission charge), when a very pleasant lady on the reception desk said, "Do have a look upstairs, it's really very good."

I thanked her and headed for the stairs, and do you know what? She was right; it was exceptional. The exhibits traced the story of Buxton and surrounding areas from the Ice Age, through to the Romans, Saxons, Victorians and finally present-day Buxton. The whole exhibition was set out with darkened passages and scary corners with authentic scenes and smells. The whole place was packed with artefacts, among which were, trilobites, fossils, Roman coins and even the leg bone of a sabre-tooth tiger. So eerie was the whole experience that one little chap in front of me simply buried his head inside his grandmother's coat for the whole duration of the visit. I on the other hand had nowhere to hide, so I manfully toughed it out. Once away from the spooky bits, the exhibition culminated in the Tomlinson Collection, 'the world's finest collection of Ashford Black Marble'. There are approximately 150 pieces of this unusual polished ware, from clocks to plates, and letter openers to mirrors – it had the lot. If you are into geology and archaeology then the final exhibits are for you. For here, in this unique museum you can trace the life and times of the eminent geologist William Boyd Dawkins, 1837-1929, curator of the natural history department of the Manchester Museum, and an all-round clever bod.

Passing my friend on the reception desk, I smiled. "You were right, it's very good indeed."

Isn't everywhere so much nicer when the sun comes out to play? Down the hill I strolled in the direction of New Buxton, but not before passing Potter's general clothing store. Here I stopped and gazed in pure awe at the window displays, for here on show were 101 things I thought had long since disappeared off any modern day shopping list. There were long socks (and I mean long), Panama hats, knickers of a voluminous size and a myriad of quirky items crammed into this wonderful time warp shop. The original Edwardian façade, only added to the whole dotty experience. I hope they survive forever.

When I say I headed towards New Buxton, it is only new in relation to the old Buxton. In historical terms, a great deal of the beautiful architecture to be seen in this area of the town dates back to the mid Georgian period, so is not in fact new at all. The principal architect of the New Buxton was the Fifth Duke of Devonshire, who developed the classic Neo-Georgian 'Crescent' along with several other worthy buildings. Set in a perfect arc it was completed in 1788 and featured a huge ballroom and assembly rooms. Originally the building contained a beautiful town house for the exclusive use of the Cavendish family, and was used when visiting town from nearby Chatsworth, the family seat. By 1804 the Duke relinquished his accommodation and it became a trio of hotels – the Centre Hotel, with the St Ann's hotel to the west, and the Great Hotel to the east. Around this time (1790), the Duke also built the wonderful domed-top stables (more anon). The crescent is currently empty and is partially hidden up to first-floor level by mesh grills, decorated with information hoardings explaining the intended future use of this fine building.

Directly across the road from the crescent there is a small stone monument, and in the middle of a flat plaque sits a solid brass tap, from which you can draw the natural spring water. Which is exactly what one lady was doing with great relish. Equipped with two large Sainsbury's 'Bags For Life' and approximately twelve empty water bottles she was busy filling up her supply of Buxton water.

Always the curious one, I asked her why she chose this natural alternative.

"Well, it's free for a start, but more than that, it's pure."

"Why – what's its source?" I asked.

"It comes from the Derbyshire hills and it's said that it takes over a thousand years to reach this point." A thousand years, I pondered; King Harold had still got two eyes, Henry VIII was not even a twinkle, and Katie Price was secreted deep in Essex working on her first novel.

"Does it taste different to the other waters readily available?"

"Try it."

I cupped both hands and sipped on the clear liquid. I have to admit it was very pleasant, there was no real aftertaste, but neither was there anything unpleasant. We continued in conversation as she filled the seventh bottle, and she told me what had brought her to the well originally.

"I had a stomach complaint that had become gradually worse. I'd seen countless doctors and had every type of test known to modern medicine, when a friend suggested I try this water." Her face changed into a look of revelation. "Within two months all my pain and discomfort had vanished. That was four years ago. Now I wouldn't dare use normal drinking water."

"Are there any generally-known benefits associated with the water?"

"Well, it's said it does have a fairly high radioactive content."

"You're not glowing in the dark yet then?" I quipped.

"No not yet, and my teeth haven't fallen out either."

I said goodbye and left this very chatty lady to her H_2O production line.

Among the many charms that Buxton displays to its annual influx of visitors, none is more appealing than its Opera House. Designed by the great theatre architect Frank Matcham, who also designed The London Palladium (1910) and the London Coliseum (1904), the Buxton Opera House opened to great acclaim in 1903 – it is a little gem. So technically perfect was Matcham's stage and lighting set up that it attracted much of the top echelon of British talent for the next three decades including the Old Vic, various Shakespeare companies, musical comedies, ballet and a host of famous names, including, Alec Guiness, Sybil Thorndike, Robert Morley, Robert Donat, Anthony Quayle and the great Anna Pavlova, who performed the Dance of the Dying Swan. The venue remained purely as a theatre until around 1927 when it was adapted to mixed use as a theatre/cinema. It achieved a degree of success as a cinema through the fifties and sixties, but by the seventies it was clear that the Opera House was becoming more difficult to maintain. As the audiences dwindled, so the theatre fell into disrepair until it was temporarily closed in October 1976. Something had to be done and quickly, and there followed three years of dedicated work and fundraising, during which time the Opera House was lovingly restored. In 1979 the little theatre proudly opened its doors once more. Despite its compact appearance the Opera House is very deceptive, it seats 946 people and the newly-extended orchestra pit can accommodate up to eighty-five musicians and boasts a stage large enough to host grand opera.

The interior is a triumph of high theatre art. Matcham used many styles in the design of this prettiest of theatres, but somehow they all blend into a pleasing fusion. Here Art Nouveau, sits alongside the cleaner Edwardian lines of the upper circle with complete ease. The original colour scheme was uncovered during restoration and has been adhered to wherever possible, and in the central domed ceiling a huge gas-fired sun burner has been restored (modified to run on North Sea Gas no less).

As a provincial theatre it has few equals in condition, practicality and utter charm. Each year the town of Buxton hosts a festival of the arts and an integral part of this celebration is always the varied programme offered by this Theatre. I recommend a visit.

The Buxton Opera House is in essence the picturesque frontispiece for a much larger complex, the Pavilion and Pavilion Gardens. The original nine-acre plot of land was a gift from the Duke of Devonshire to the people of Buxton (this was extended in due course to twenty-three acres by way of Ducal gifts). They were to be, 'held in perpetuity on condition they were used exclusively for the purposes of such gardens and pleasure grounds'. The eminent landscape gardener Edward Milner was appointed, and the gardens were officially opened on 11th May 1871. Followed in very short order by the opening of the Pavilion. The Concert Hall or Pavilion was designed by local architect Robert Rippon Duke, and was completed in 1875. It is a wonderful high Victorian, octagonal showpiece. Originally known as the Pavilion Theatre, it later became the Hippodrome (cinema) and home to the Buxton Gardens

Theatre Company who were instrumental in pushing for a new, more purpose-built venue – hence the Opera House. Connected by an ornate Victorian, cast-iron and glass conservatory, the Pavilion is used nowadays for a multitude of events, from antique fairs to brass band concerts and art exhibitions to farmers' markets.

In what is a masterclass in landscaping and horticultural good sense, the Pavilion Gardens are a credit to the people of Buxton. Here you can step back to a more tranquil age and enjoy the timeless appearance of the gardens, play a game of mini golf, or as many of the youngsters on this bright day were doing, ride the miniature railway that snakes through this delightful acreage – accompanied by fathers who seemed more delighted than their children to have the opportunity to ride this mini-rail. Looking at the gardens from a vantage point near the Pavilion, the shrubbery appeared sublime and the flowers dramatic, and all this comes with a free entrance tag. Thank you, Buxton.

Buxton is a grand little town, and I mean that not in a patronising way, but purely as a reference to its impressive architecture. Around every corner another joy or surprise awaits you. From the Crescent to the Pump Rooms, the Opera House to the Pavilion, there is always a new treat in store, and the Devonshire Stables were no exception. Set proudly on a hill to the west of the town sits the former stabling block of the Duke of Devonshire. The phrase 'stabling block' is in this case misleading in the extreme. What you see before you is the most glorious dome-topped, circular stone-built statement of its age. Built once again by his grace The Duke of Devonshire (he got about a bit), in 1785 the building was originally used as a home for some 110 horses, serving not only the Duke's needs but also those of the nearby crescent, a sort of latter-day NCP. In a typical act of Cavendish largesse, in 1859 the 6th Duke gave the stables to a charitable trust, on the strict understanding that it would be converted into a hospital. The architect Henry Curry was appointed to design a cover for the circular exercise area. He came up with what at the time was the largest unsupported dome in the world. In actual fact, only two-thirds of the building were gifted for use as a hospital – one third remaining as a working stable until 1881 when this too was adapted to hospital needs. A clock tower and lodge were built in 1882; in 1897 surgical wards were added, followed by the hydro spa baths in 1913. The timing was perfect, for less than twelve months later Britain was at war. The hospital was drafted into service, and to get a feel of this dramatic building during those dark days, you can do no better than read this extract from one of Buxton's most notable daughters Vera Brittain, taken from her book *Testament of Youth*:

> *On Sunday morning, June 7th, 1915, I began my nursing at the Devonshire Hospital. The same date, exactly ten years afterwards, was to be, for me, equally memorable. Between the one day and the other lies the rest of this book.*
>
> *From our house above the town I ran eagerly downhill to my first morning's work, not knowing, fortunately for myself, that my servitude would last for nearly four years. The hospital had originally been used as a riding-school, but a certain Duke of Devonshire, with exemplary concern for the welfare of the sick but none whatever for the feet of the nursing staff, had caused it to be converted to its present charitable purpose. The main part of the building consisted of a huge dome, with two stone corridors running one above the other round its quarter-mile circumference. The nurses were not allowed to cross its diameter, which contained an inner circle reserved for convalescent patients, so that everything forgotten or newly required meant a run round the circumference. As kitchens, sink-rooms and*

*wards all led off the circular corridors and appeared to
have been built as far from one another as possible, the
continuous walking along the un-resistant stone floors
must have amounted, apart from the work itself, to
several miles a day.*

*My hours there ran from 7.45 am until 1 pm, and
again from 5.00 pm until 9.15 pm – a longer day, as
I afterwards discovered, than that normally required
in many Army hospitals. No doubt the staff was not
unwilling to make the utmost use of so enthusiastic
and unsophisticated a probationer. Meals, for all of
which I was expected to go home, were not included
in these hours. As our house was nearly half a mile
from the hospital on the slope of a steep hill, I never
completely overcame the aching of my back and the
soreness of my feet throughout the time that I worked
there, and felt perpetually as if I had just returned
from a series of long route marches.*

I walked the short distance from the pavilion gardens to the
Devonshire, as it is still lovingly known locally. Despite its success as
a hydrotherapy unit within the NHS and its reputation for effective
treatment of many arthritic ailments, the hospital closed its doors
in 2000. In 2001 the University of Derby took over control of the
building and began work on the conversion to a place of learning.
The first students were enrolled in 2005 and by the amount of young
people milling around this day, I think the same enrolment process
was in full swing. Appearing a little older than the average student
on campus, I thought it may be difficult to blag it and simply walk
past the security booth, so I explained my intentions to the very
pleasant lady in the box.

"No problem, take as long as you like, but if you could keep to
the outer corridor while the enrolment is going on."

"Thank you, do you get many visitors?" I asked.

"We do get a few, but I think most people are put off when they see the security. The keenest ones though are the Japanese, they just love the place. Here's a leaflet and if you have any further questions, I'm sure we can find someone to answer them for you."

Is it me or is this country full of the most helpful people in the world? This lady spends her working day inside an eight foot square box and she is politeness personified. Others get paid a King's ransom for doing very little and couldn't give a stuff. The pamphlet gave a brief history of the building's unique past and its place in the future of this Derbyshire spa town. The leaflet was entitled *From Horses to Courses*. Can we get one thing straight, you concentrate on the education of the young, I'll do the play on words!

Well, this is something else. The moment you pass through the large impressive entrance doors you know you are viewing something very special and totally unique. The huge ceiling is supported by impressive metal struts that lead in a perfect arc from their first floor base to a breathtaking cathedral-like glass topped dome. At ground and first level, a circular gallery leads to a multitude of rooms. These were obviously once the separate rooms that adjoined the central ward; now, instead of the sick and infirm, the place buzzes with the joyful sound of young students, bright, happy people, their whole future ahead of them, barely aware of the rich history that daily surrounds them – and why should they be? Appreciation of the finer things is for old gits like me.

I had become fascinated with the story of Vera Brittain, but could find little record of her time spent in Buxton. There was certainly no blue plaque to commemorate her efforts, and even less local information. It was well documented that Vera had little time for Buxton and only returned when she had to. She had openly said that she found the place to be narrow in outlook and rather mean-spirited, so maybe this was the ultimate revenge. Being that any visit to Buxton will leave you very little wiser as to her time spent here,

I will give you a résumé of her earlier life.

Vera Mary Brittain was born 29th December 1893 in Newcastle-under-Lyme, Staffordshire, the elder of two children. Her father Thomas Arthur Brittain, was a paper manufacturer. In 1895 Thomas moved his family to the silk manufacturing town of Macclesfield, Cheshire and in this year Vera gained a younger brother, Edward. In 1905 the Brittains moved to Buxton in Derbyshire, the then fashionable spa town. After two years attending the local Grange School, Vera was sent to St Monica's School at Kingswood in Surrey. There she fell under the powerful influence of the school's headmistress, Louise Heath-Jones. Heath-Jones was a radical and encouraged Vera to study current affairs, taking her to her to women's suffrage meetings, an experience which contributed enormously to Vera's growing feminist views. Between 1912 and 1913 while back in Buxton, Vera attended a course of Oxford University extension lectures given by the historian John Marriot. Ever the determined modern lady, Vera, due almost entirely to her own efforts, achieved an exhibition entrance to Somerville College, Oxford; her subject, English Literature. This was a precursor to the actual entrance examination, which she passed in March 1914. By the summer of that year she gained entrance to the university itself.

When war was declared in August 1914 her brother Edward and his closest friend from Uppingham School, Roland Leighton, applied for commissions in the British army. Roland was sent to the Western Front with the 7th Worcestershire regiment in the spring of 1915. He and Vera became engaged while he was on leave in August of that year. Feeling isolated from the war in her first year at Somerville, Vera soon decided to leave Oxford for the duration of the war. Anxious to play her part in what was rapidly becoming a 'bloody war', she applied to become a VAD nurse.

Returning to Buxton in June 1915, she commenced work, as previously stated at the Devonshire Hospital. Her stay here was relatively short and in November of that year she transferred to the

First London General Hospital in Camberwell.

One year later on 26 December 1915, while waiting at Brighton for Roland to return on leave, Vera learned that he had been killed by a German sniper while serving in France. In the following year her brother Edward received his commission and by chance was sent to Camberwell to recover from his injuries received at the battle of the Somme. That September Vera was given her first foreign posting in Malta. Her world was further shattered when in 1918, whilst taking time out to look after her parents, they received news of Edward's death. Vera went on to write various poetry and works, but she is best remembered for her book Testament of Youth, as well as a lifelong commitment to the peace movement.

I made my way back towards my car, once more passing St Anne's Well where they were still filling up the odd water bottles. So the next time you are stood in a public place and confronted by someone in glowing health – literally – you will know they are from Buxton.

A Little Taste of Italy

Say Cheshire to most people and they would normally think of The Cheshire Plain, serene farmland, rolling pastures, oh, and cheese. Well they would be right, for Cheshire has all of these things and so much more. It has an abundance of picturesque villages, wooded hillsides, verdant parks and a plethora of grand houses and stately homes. It also has another side less known, but equally evident to any traveller from the southern counties. If you are looking for an area that flies in the face of every preconception held about the north, then look no further than south Manchester. The areas of Hale and Knutsford in the west, to Wilmslow and Alderley Edge in the east, form what is known by local estate agents as the Golden Triangle. So distinct is this patch of Cheshire, that it would be difficult to pinpoint another region as prosperous or self- assured, other than the Thames Valley perhaps. Here houses that would match anything that could be found in Sunningdale or Virginia Water, spring up with alarming regularity. Even the latest financial downturn appears to have had little or no discernable impact, as the developers simply switch to bespoke houses rather than speculative dwellings.

I found this chapter of the book the most difficult, living as I do slap-bang in the middle of this area. I had to mentally detach myself from what could so easily have become a lazy man's trail, a sort of laconic, easy chapter. I had therefore, to adopt a newcomer's eye to what would normally be familiar territory.

Drive south out of Manchester and without warning the major dual carriageway that progresses through the city's suburbs changes almost imperceptibly into the M56 motorway. Equally noticeable is the loss of suburbia as lush green farmland and fulsome hedgerows suddenly surround you. Within less than a twenty-minute drive from the city centre you can, if the inspiration grabs you, take the turning for Chester and Knutsford. Which is exactly what I did.

Knutsford is said to derive its name from the Danish King, Canute, who supposedly forded the River Lily in 1016. The name Cunetesford appears in the Domesday Book (1086) and it doesn't take a great leap of the imagination to see how the name Knutsford came into being. There was certainly no tide to turn back on the day I arrived in Cunetesford.

On first appearance Knutsford has an easy old-world charm that belies some of its more interesting history. King Street is the main thoroughfare, presented as a narrow slip of a road, lined on both sides with an abundance of interesting and individual shops. Apart from a Costa Coffee, a Waterstone's and a Boots, there are none of the usual multiples that clutter up our high streets and make almost every town in the UK a carbon copy of the previous one. The very lack of such sameness adds a comfortable homely feel to this pretty market town. The variance of the architecture, which is principally black and white half-timbered buildings, only increases its obvious appeal.

Among the many charms that Knutsford displays to newcomers and locals alike, none is more obvious than the width of the pavements, or perhaps that should read the lack of width, along one side of King Street. They really are so narrow that it is difficult to pass anyone without stepping into the road. Any sane person would have taken this as the norm and carried on pressing the glass of the many and varied outlets, and enjoying the diversity of the wares on show. As I clearly don't fall into this category, I wondered if there was a specific reason, other than an acute shortage of paving slabs.

My curiosity was rewarded when I looked a little deeper into the origins of the teeny-tiny pavement. The paving – such as it is – was a gift to the people of Knutsford from Lady Jane Stanley, wife of the Earl of Stanley and was constructed towards the end of the 18th century. Her largesse however, was only matched by her propriety. The construction of the walkway and its subsequent upkeep were conditional on the width being maintained, ensuring the young ladies of Knutsford were unable to walk hand in hand with the 'young man of their fancy'.

What an old curmudgeon!

Any direct effect this statute had upon the birth rate of this town is not documented, but needless to say the pavement on the opposite side of the street is considerably wider.

The narrowness of the pavement became an added worry when every other building for the first two-hundred yards or so along King Street became a complete distraction in its own right. Principal amongst which was the Gaskell Tower – a wonderful Italianate structure designed by Richard Harding Watt in celebration of the author Elizabeth Gaskell, and now the home of the La Belle Époque restaurant. Harding Watt was born in Manchester around 1842 (not specified in records). He became a glove merchant whose passion and obvious architectural influence came via his travels while on business in France and Italy. Thwarted in his attempt to marry Ethel Armitage, the daughter of a wealthy local builder, the love of his life and twenty years his junior, he set out on his quest to import a little bit of Italy into rural Cheshire. Due in no small measure to the intransigence of the Armitage family, he had to wait for the best part of two decades to win the hand of their beloved daughter. Far from being impressed by these wonderful buildings – some say built in her honour – Ethel thought them 'silly and a waste of good money'. However it is documented that she was more than willing to collect the rents from these properties following her husband's death. Not so silly after all, eh?

There are several of these unusual buildings concealed around Knutsford; one in particular could be called the daddy of them all. The building in question is The Ruskin Rooms with adjoining cottages and laundry building. Watt made no secret of his admiration for the writer and art critic John Ruskin, and in the most blatant act of sycophancy imaginable, even included extracts from the great man's work literally carved in stone around his buildings.

The one over the main door of the Ruskin Rooms reads as follows:

> *Let every dawn of morning*
> *be to you as the beginning of*
> *life and every setting sun*
> *be to you as its close*
> *John Ruskin*

Had I been blindfolded, spun round the obligatory three times and placed outside The Ruskin Rooms, I would have bet a month's salary that I had been magically transported to San Gimignano. So Italian in flavour is this building and the adjoining buildings along Drury Lane, that on this sunny day in August all I needed was a cool glass of Pinot Grigio and Knutsford would have become the base for my Dolce Vita.

Harding Watt, it appears, was one of the early pioneers of recycling. In common with that other great salvager Sir Clough Williams Ellis (of Port Meirion fame) Harding Watt was an assiduous collector of pediments, arches, cornerstones and the like. He salvaged much of his impressive adornments from large houses, churches and factories across many northern counties. He may not have been a hit with the in-laws, but my goodness his erections were impressive.

Knutsford has an easy grace, and in common with so many of

the UK's towns and villages, has a history that is inextricably linked to the nearby manor house or stately home. In Knutsford's case that link is Tatton Park, the ancestral home of the Egerton family.

The entrance to Tatton Park is a mere 150 yards from the top of King Street. Passing under the gateway and entrance kiosk – free for walkers, £5 for cars – I decided this boy was walking. Once within the park you are met by the longest driveway imaginable. If in days gone by, they had sent a footman out to brush the drive in November, he wouldn't have returned until Christmas!

The sun was bright, the clouds fluffy, and a warm wind was blowing in from the south. The vista was one of uninterrupted parkland as far as the eye could see, and the whole tranquil scene completed by lazy deer and a stag with the most enormous antlers, that were totally disproportionate to his sleek body. For a fleeting moment it reminded me of a Landseer painting, something like *The Stag at Bay*, only in this painting, the deep heather strewn glen had been replaced by verdant pasture and ancient oak trees.

For the best part of forty minutes I trudged along the never-ending driveway, as happy people in their Range Rovers breezed past, their children (as they watched from the rear window) giving their parents questioning looks as to why someone would walk all this way.

Because I'm saving five ponds, that's why! Not that we writers are careful with money or anything, but it does seem to go with the territory. Maybe I'll try being an Member of Parliament next time round, they're not stuck for a fiver or two.

After a further leg-sapping ten minutes I reached the front gates of Tatton Hall, and what a pretty sight it was. A splendid Neo-Classical house, designed for Lord Egerton by Thomas Wyatt. The house was commissioned in 1770 and completed in the early 1800s. Sadly both Lord Egerton and Wyatt died before the house was completed. And you thought you had to wait a long time for your builder to finish a job. This is not a grand house in the manner of Chatsworth but is no less impressive for its more diminutive size. Set in 25,000 acres of rolling parkland it is still one hunk of real estate.

I meandered alongside the perimeter wall until I came to the stable block, now tastefully converted into tearooms, a gift shop, a garden shop and a house museum extension. Tatton was the seat of the Egerton family from 1598 until 1958 (did you notice that the two dates are made up of exactly the same numbers?) when Maurice Egerton (a bachelor) died. With no heir to carry on the great house or name, it was bequeathed to the National Trust. Is it just me or do the gift buyers for the National Trust only visit gift fairs with a time line of 1960? The sum total of everything sold through their numerous outlets must make up the basic content of at least two bottom drawers in every UK household. I didn't need a hedgehog foot scraper or a tea towel extolling the virtues of Tatton or anywhere else, so I settled on a pack of Egerton Mints. At least they would not be unearthed by my nearest and dearest after I've shuffled off this mortal coil.

What the gift shop lacked in sparkling content, the tearooms more than made up for. Sat at a picnic-style table under a warming sun, I tucked into a cappuccino and a scone with enough jam and cream to clog several arteries – but who cares? I for one am sick of being told what I can and can't eat, tired of feeling guilty for driving, flying, having one too many glasses of wine, and not placing bottles in the right-coloured bin. I'm tired of being filmed on CCTV without my permission, and utterly fed up with nanny-state politicians who don't practice what they preach! Sorry, I don't know where that came from, but the scone was wonderful.

Looking around this very tranquil walled courtyard and my fellow scoffers it struck me just how much we Brits enjoy the smallest of pleasures. Not for us are the grand gestures, the theatrical pavement cafés or the prancing Italian waiter. No, give the average Brit a good cuppa, hazy sunshine, a mellow garden and a scone, and I'll show you a contented fellow – as long as we can have an ice-cream on the way home.

Tatton Hall really is a joy and by the third room or so I could almost envisage living here. The rooms were obviously grand by any modern-day standard, but nothing felt so huge as to be uncomfortable. At Christmas time the house plays host to festive parties, where people join in the themed atmosphere by dressing up in Victorian costume and devouring banquet meals with drink aplenty. I would happily attend such a gathering as long as I could be guaranteed a four-poster bed for the evening. It really is a very attractive house. The one thing that always strikes me when I visit such places as Tatton, is the obvious disparity of wealth they exhibited in their heyday. Being at the top of the tree must have been sublime, but God help you if you were mucking out the stables. I'm sure estate jobs must have had some benefits over millwork perhaps, but the daily reminder of how your 'betters' were living couldn't have been easy.

The Egertons were great hunters, as witnessed in the long gallery, where countless stuffed heads of various prey are eerily mounted on plaques along the length of the high walls. There is something vaguely disconcerting about seeing an animal without its body – obviously an acquired taste. Not in question however, was the Italian terraced garden and fernery created by Joseph Paxton (of Crystal Palace fame). The more I saw of this pretty house, the more I envisaged having my post redirected to this address. Within forty minutes or so I was passing back through the arched gateway that led me back to King Street. A thoroughly enjoyable three hours or so had passed and don't forget, I'd saved a fiver!

Thanks to the television series of *Cranford*, the name of Elizabeth Gaskell has been brought once more to our attention. For those of you who may not be aware, the novel *Cranford* was based on Knutsford, the one-time home of Elizabeth. Across a broad heath – the site of the local racecourse up until 1873 –sits the pretty Queen Anne house where Miss Gaskell lived with her aunt, Hannah Lumb.

Elizabeth had been brought to Knutsford from London, following the death of her mother in October 1811. She was just thirteen months old when she arrived at what was to be her hometown and the setting for her best-known work – Cranford.

Knutsford around the time of Elizabeth's eighth birthday was rapidly expanding. A new Palladian-fronted courthouse was under construction, and the town was prosperous and semi-genteel. The general chatter of both the residents of Knutsford and her extended family formed the perfect backdrop and a wealth of inspiration for the budding author.

Elizabeth went on to marry William Gaskell, a minister and leading light within the Unitarian church. She moved to a very smart house on what was then the outskirts of Manchester. Although her most famous novel was *Cranford*, her true talent shone through when in 1854 she wrote *North and South*, a gritty work based on the inequities of the class system of the time. With the support of friends like Charles Dickens (also her publisher) and the Brontë sisters, she was not afraid to ruffle a few feathers, even within her own comfortable social circle. Elizabeth wasn't blessed with a long life as she died on November 12th 1865, aged just fifty-five and was buried in a simple plot within the grounds of the Unitarian Church on Brook Street, Knutsford.

The house today looks surprisingly similar to how it would have done in Elizabeth's day – a perfect timeless façade facing a wide-open heath land. I think she would approve. Which is probably more than the present occupants do when faced with the constant flow of Cranford devotees, and strange-looking men of a certain age who stand near your front gate, writing copious notes and smiling back at you when you pull back the net curtains to see who's lurking outside your fine home. Sorry I meant no harm.

I crossed the road (re-named Gaskell Avenue) to the heath, or as it is now more widely known, Knutsford Common. You may have seen this green space and not even realised it, for although as previously stated this was once a racecourse, another race was held some years ago which grabbed all the national headlines. This was the spot where Martin Bell (or the 'Man in The White Suit'), met the local MP Neil Hamilton in a by-election debate. Bell's anti-sleaze ticket was gathering momentum, when he was challenged by Mr Hamilton to hold a face-to-face meeting on Knutsford Common. What would have usually passed for another political debate or at least a heated argument, developed into farce when Neil arrived with his wife, and self-confessed 'battle-axe', Christine. Any composure Martin Bell had shown up until this moment evaporated when Christine verbally hand-bagged him. It was lousy politics, but great TV. By chance, some months later I was invited to a dinner dance at Astra Zenica's Alderley Park, where the guest of honour was none other than Martin Bell. During his after-dinner speech he regaled us with tales of his work as a BBC correspondent during the Balkans war, and told us how he came to be wounded by a sniper's bullet.

He concluded, "Although I have had a lifetime of scary situations and found myself in places I would rather have not been – nothing compared to the feeling of dread I felt that day on Knutsford Common, and the venomous attack by Christine Hamilton." You have been warned. Don't mess with the women-folk of Knutsford!

Knutsford today is a pleasant and picturesque town, and unlike so many places where a famous person or event is lauded on every street sign or honoured on every shop facia, Knutsford has very few references to either Elizabeth Gaskell or Cranford. Save for one rather smart looking sandwich bar that carries the Cranford brand, and the white bust of Elizabeth that adorns the Gaskell Tea Rooms, you would hardly know that this was the home of their most famous daughter. I liked that; restraint has its own rewards.

The day was still fine as I made my way to the outer edges of Knutsford, passing the impressive Assize Courts on my right. I'd forgotten that Knutsford had a major criminal court, and had played host to some rather high-profile cases. One of the more unusual ones I unearthed was that of Alan Turing, the brilliant mathematician, a huge contributor to Britain's war effort via Bletchley Park, and a key player in breaking the enigma code. Widely regarded as the father of the modern computer, he was – by his own admission – gay. This was a time when the only gay activity that was actively encouraged was the pursuit of happiness. So it was in March 1952 that he was brought before the courts on a charge of homosexuality. He was found guilty as charged, but instead of a custodial sentence he agreed to undergo hormone therapy for a period of twelve months. A treatment that was rumoured to have led to abnormal pectorals, which on a man of Turing's slight stature were said, 'to have strongly resembled female breasts'. Great! You help crack the Enigma code and save your country from the march of the German jackboot, and what do they give you in return? A pair of boobs! Turing's plight became even more desperate, when it became commonly held in certain circles that he was, for some obscure reason, considered a serious security risk. Turing paid the ultimate price, when in June 1954 he died from cyanide poisoning. A verdict of suicide was returned.

The more I delved into the history of this quirky town, the more amazed I became by just who had visited. Passing the old Town Hall, with its wonderful Gothic-style façade – now a furniture shop and post office – I was reminded that one General George Patton had delivered a speech here, which effectively ended any post-war political ambitions he may have had. On April 25th 1944, Patton made a speech that became known as the 'Knutsford Incident'. Speaking to the soldiers attending the opening of the Knutsford Welcome Club, Patton made his brief introduction and made a few throwaway remarks.Then without warning he delivered the following line: "It is the evident destiny of the British and Americans and, of course, the Russians, to rule the world."

His remarks were seized upon by newspapers on both sides of the Atlantic. Unfortunately they omitted the Russians, thereby slighting one of our main allies. All those present that day insisted he had included the Russians, but as we all know, a lie travels halfway around the world while the truth is struggling to get out of the next county. Churchill was by all accounts furious, castigating the swaggering cigar-smoking general in no uncertain terms. Sound a little like the pot calling the kettle black?

It was time to move on, but before I exited the boundaries of this pleasant town I had one more place to visit – Leigh Road. It was once described as the 'craziest road in the whole of England', a title earned thanks yet again to our old friend Richard Harding Watt. His 'madcap' scheme was to build eight Mediterranean-style villas along the length of Leigh Road. This area had long since been the premier area of Knutsford, with huge houses set in impressive grounds along the left-hand side of this tree-lined avenue. Watt spotted an opportunity to build on the adjacent land sloping down to the Lily. Undeterred by the natural elevation of the building plots and local opposition in general, Watt pushed on.

I walked the half-mile or so to Leigh Road and, sure enough, sat at a luxurious distance back from the kerb were Wyatt's Villas.

What villas they are! Each one individual but somehow harmoniously linked to its neighbour. How much these prime pieces of property are now worth I wouldn't like to guess, but you could rest assured that the price tag would include several noughts. I walked the length of Leigh Road and stood slack-jawed at several of the gated entrances to the rear of each property, and impressive trees and shrubs reduced in stature as they obviously cascaded to the river below. The houses carried wonderfully romantic names like: Chantry Dane, Lake House and Breeze.

The relative tranquillity of Leigh Road was momentarily disturbed in 1987 when Steven Spielberg rolled into town and transformed this affluent residential thoroughfare into colonial Shanghai for the opening sequence of his epic film *Empire of The Sun*, based on the work of J.G.Ballard and his boyhood experiences during the Japanese occupation of Shanghai. Bamboo fences were erected outside these grand houses, and for a brief time, Japanese armoured carriers trundled menacingly up and down Leigh Road. The only lasting reminder of such heady days are the bamboo fences that many owners decided were a welcome addition to their property, and so left them in situ once Spielberg had departed.

Despite the criticism Harding Watt endured during his lifetime, he was known to be immensely pleased with his contribution to the overall appearance of Knutsford. In particular the balance he felt he had achieved with the Gaskell Tower and its counterpoint, the minarets of the laundry building on Drury Lane. So enamoured was he with his achievements, that he was known to stand up in his carriage whenever he approached Knutsford to effect a clearer view. They say pride comes before a fall, and in a strange twist of irony, one day in 1913 he stood up as usual on his approach to town, the horse shied and he was thrown from his carriage and subsequently died.

'Watt' an untimely ending!

Wizards and WAGS

The road from Knutsford to Wilmslow is a very familiar one to me. A mere eight miles or so of winding lanes and lush farmland separate the two towns. There, all comparison stops. Where Knutsford is graced with old buildings and narrow streets, Wilmslow is posh suburbia. Here football managers, footballers and soap stars rub shoulders with mere mortals like me, on a daily basis. The town is neat and cared for with a wide mix of retail activity, from the usual multiples like Smiths and Superdrug to the upmarket Hoopers department store, two very expensive jewellers and a wonderful showroom full of stunning Aston Martin cars – a little out of my price range, unless of course you encourage everyone you know to rush out and buy this book immediately.

Not more than five minutes from my home – so I could nip home for a quick coffee on this one – sits the very beautiful and unique Styal country park and the equally disarming Styal village. This is also the home of one of the most enlightened mill complexes of the late 18th and early 19th century – Quarry Bank Mill. Founded by Samuel Greg, born in 1758, the second son of Thomas Greg and Elizabeth Hyde of Belfast. His father was a successful merchant and ship-owner. His mother's family were also wealthy business people. The family had strong connections with Manchester via Elizabeth's brother Robert Hyde, who was a very successful merchant based in the city. He imported linen yarns from Ireland and used Lancashire weavers to turn it into finished cloth. This was in turn exported to Europe or America.

Following a rigorous private education, Samuel Greg joined his uncle's company in Manchester and by 1780 became a junior partner. Within two years Robert Hyde had died and Thomas took over what was now a very substantial firm. The cloth stock alone stood at £26,000.

Within three years of running the company it became clear to Samuel that he desperately needed more quality yarn. There seemed little possibility of securing a regular supply, so to Samuel the solution was simple – he would build his own textile mill. After surveying several sites for his new venture, he stumbled upon a deep, wooded valley near Styal in Cheshire. The fact that the fast-flowing River Bollin followed a natural elevation through the valley convinced him that he could also power his mill for a very economical sum – and so Quarry Bank Mill was founded.

The mill was completed around 1784 at a cost of £3,000, and initially employed around 150 men spinning coarse yarn on water frames, powered by a huge waterwheel deep under the mill, ingeniously fed from the River Bollin. In 1879 Samuel married Hannah Lightbody, the daughter of a Unitarian cotton merchant and someone who was to have a profound effect upon the whole humane aspect of mill ownership. With her, Hannah brought her father's strong religious beliefs and a handy dowry of £10,000, a huge sum for that period. This was used to renew the waterwheel and build cottages for the workers, who were now being brought in from Manchester, and surrounding areas, so accommodation was vital.

I drove the half mile or so along the approach road to Quarry Bank Mill, until I came to the obligatory entrance kiosk. Here I was relieved of the standard entrance fee of £4.50 for the grounds only. Dumping my car in the very crowded carpark, I descended the steep steps that lead to the mill. Here there was a further booking office where I was relieved of a further crisp ten pound note for the mill and Apprentices House tour – £14.50 in total – I ask you, although I suppose they have to find the money for all those tea towels from somewhere. I noticed, when reading some of the blurb that came with the modest entrance fee, that the whole restoration project for the mill had, over many years, received royal approval and support in the form of non other than HRH Princess Anne. I wonder how she paid? "Do you accept these notes with pictures of Mummy on them?"

I set off to get my money's worth – honestly the money I have to spend to bring you factual information! The setting is nothing less than glorious, and the restoration, obviously completed over a great number of years, a total credit to all concerned. I flashed my priceless ticket to the volunteer manning the main entrance and entered Mr Greg's hallowed creation via a first-level gantry.

The mill tour starts upside-down, so to speak. You enter at the fourth level and proceed downwards. The first two levels were laid out in great detail, everything from the origins of the cotton tree, through to a full demonstration on a wooden-framed hand loom by a grey-haired lady with rosy cheeks, suitably attired in period clothing. One display in particular caught my eye, and I passed a good ten minutes absorbing the information. The section in question detailed the various jobs and skills that were carried out on a daily basis within a typical cotton mill. Here are just some of the wonderful job titles: drawers and rovers, mixers, carders, warpers, beamers, mule-spinners and the simply wonderful throstle-spinners; that's got to add a certain caché to any CV. Passing through the hands-on section of the museum – you know, the part where every child under the age of ten is let loose for fifteen minutes, so the rest of us can go on ahead and enjoy the tour – I proceeded to a lower floor. Here I got the first glimpse of the real thing, a huge expanse of weaving machines, loaded with reels and ready for action but strangely silent. What it must have been like when twenty or so of these things were rattling away at once, heaven only knows – but I was about to find out. For there, in all their noisy glory on the floor below, six of the twenty or so beasts were weaving at full tilt. And guess what they were weaving – that's right, the linen cloth for the Quarry Bank tea towels.

I stopped to talk to Rex, the man responsible for these noisy looms. Removing his ear-defenders and temporarily silencing the machinery, he answered all my questions with enthusiasm and authority. Rex had obviously done this a hundred times before, but had that rare gift of making you feel that you were the first recipient of such erudition. Within less than five minutes, my monopoly on Rex was lost to a gathering crowd, principal among which was a Liverpudlian of such obvious militant tendencies, that he almost appeared to hold Rex personally responsible for the fact that in the early 1800s children as young as six were working a twelve-hour day, six days a week. Not until the Factory Act of 1850 did the recruiting of children for such tedious hard work become less financially beneficial to the 'wicked mill owners'. Despite the better-than-average living conditions and a degree of social welfare shown for their workers, the Gregs were not adverse to some rather stringent conditions if it kept the balance sheet bright. As late as 1834 they were still vehemently opposing employment reform on the basis that shorter working hours would cause rising prices leading to more unemployment – the oldest gripe in the book.

My Scouse friend became almost apoplectic when he was told by Rex that the workers were locked in at the start of the day. The doors were only unlocked for their half-hour lunch break, then re-locked until 8pm. This seemed as good an opportunity as any to go and view the giant waterwheel, so I thanked Rex profusely and left Derek Hatton's brother to his rant.

When the sign said that, 'this was at one time, the largest industrial waterwheel in the world', I thought this was an idle boast. Having descended yet another flight of stairs and now viewing the wheel side-on, it was indeed huge. Originally built in 1807 and subsequently restored to working condition, it is in fact fifteen feet in diameter and a whopping ten feet wide. Let me try and put that into some form of perspective – that's twice the height of the ceiling in your living room and wider than Jo Brand!

I rounded off my visit to Quarry Bank Mill by clambering down a set of metal steps, crouching through a narrow tunnel, and following the instructions on a metal plate to stick my head skywards and view daylight at the top of a tall chimney. Being the obedient fool that I am, this is exactly what I did, and do you know what I saw? That's right – daylight. I lingered at the top of the steel steps, just to make sure I wasn't the only one that day to readily follow such strange instructions – and guess what? Every man-jack who followed me did the same – talk about sheep !

Back in the warm sunshine I sidled over to the gift shop, felt the tea towels – very nice – and purchased a small book on Styal and the mill. Then I walked next door for an ice-cream, and this brought my total spend at Quarry Bank to £21. This can't go on.

The Apprentice House is a good walk from the mill and as I'd already paid for the experience I shuffled off in that direction. The number of apprentices working in the mill at any one time varied between sixty and eighty-five; all had to be fed and boarded. A superintendent and his wife were charged with the welfare of these youngsters, in addition, a doctor was available for any sickness or injury. Looking at the Apprentice House from a 21st century perspective, we would consider the place to be cramped and basic. Adopt a 19th century view for a moment and, in comparison with the squalor found within the slums of Manchester, these were probably near-utopian conditions. Looking at the wages for 1833 it is little wonder the mill owners prospered. A child up to the age of thirteen could expect to earn the bountiful sum of between one and three shillings for a seventy-two hour week. I didn't want to be around when the

Liverpudlian discovered this unpleasant fact. Time to go I think.

I'd always intended to leave my next destination until the last. This is a village in which I spent eight happy years, and still feel is one of the nicest places in Cheshire, if not the northwest. That place is Alderley Edge.

Walk or drive through Alderley Edge on a warm summer's evening and you could be forgiven for thinking you had somehow stumbled across an extension to the Geneva motor show or a film shoot for an up-market soap opera – called *WAGs on the Edge* or something similar. Actually I quite like that title, remember where you heard it first. You would of course be totally wrong, for this is a village that plays host to south Manchester's rich and not always so famous. The most popular restaurants all have canopied pavement areas. Here young and old alike are drawn to the softly lit eateries like moths to a flame This has become the natural home of the WAGs – but Alderley has always been about so much more than flashy motors or money. The story of Alderley Edge is one of wizards and sorcery, mystery and copper mines, cotton barons and Arthurian legends.

Alderley Edge as we see it today only came into being with the arrival of the railway in 1842. The area was previously known as Chorley. This, the Manchester & Birmingham Railway Company thought, would be too easily confused with Chorley in Lancashire. So it was that the name Alderley Edge came into common use. Placed as it was at the crossroads of the old turnpike road from Manchester to Congleton, the new station would effectively be midway between the old villages of Alderley and Wilmslow. What was needed was a completely new village to compliment the link. The railway company met with Thomas Ayres, the agent for the De Traffords (the principal landowners of the area between Wilmslow and Alderley) and agreed on what we would today call a development plan. The railway company agreed to open up a station and also to build an impressive hotel alongside. In return Sir Thomas De Trafford and his agent would offer two and three acre plots for quality development. In addition, the TMBRC offered a further sweetener by offering a free first-class pass to the head of each household, providing the new home in Alderley Edge was over a certain value. The other prominent family within the area, the Stanleys, were not so easily swayed. They owned the Edge and most of the land up to and including Alderley Park, their ancestral seat. Far more traditional in outlook, they kept a discreet distance as Chorley rapidly took on its new identity – Alderley Edge. The Stanleys held fast for several decades so all development, in effect, traced the boundaries of the De Trafford land.

The opening of the station and the line to Crewe opened up the whole of south Manchester, and it soon became apparent to the 'cotton barons' and wealthy professional classes of Manchester, that Alderley might be a very pleasant place to live. The steep elevation provided by the high sandstone edge was perfect for developing the secluded villas we see today, as they offered both maximum privacy and unrivalled views over the Cheshire Plain.

As so often happens in life, the good things are soon seized upon by those who can afford them. Alderley Edge was no exception; as the stunning villas became ever more popular with the emerging higher middle class, the lower orders followed to satisfy their needs. They fell into two distinct groups, the shopkeepers who opened their various premises along the length of London Road complete with neat gardens to the front, and the workers, servants from the big houses, and miners from the nearby copper-mines, who gravitated to the small cottages that backed onto the new rail link. And so the hierarchical boundaries were set.

The main villas are set across two parallel roads – Macclesfield Road and the quieter Woodbrook Road. I decided upon the latter. Woodbrook Road, an unadopted, cobble-set thoroughfare, is littered with cavernous potholes and alarmingly steep-sided sandstone walls, that leave little room for a pedestrian to dodge a bouncing 4x4 vehicle – perfect for keeping the riff-raff away. The hill was vertically challenging in the hot midday sun, but my reward came via glimpses of the impressive dwellings, most of them, sad to say, now shielded behind high gates and impenetrable hedges. Half way up the incline the Cedars (fomerly Firwood) came into view. It was originally designed by John Gregan for John Heugh, a wealthy Scottish merchant and shipper. Even today the Cedars looks stunning, a symmetrical villa in cream brick, with a perfect high, Italianate tower – reminiscent of Osbourne House on the Isle of Wight. In 1906 Firwood became the home of the Pilkington family. They were related to the De Traffords and originally from Lancashire, founders of the Pilkington Brick and Tile Company – now of course more commonly associated with the manufacture of specialist glass.

The Pilkingtons were held in high regard by their neighbours, even if they were somewhat unconventional. One of the daughters, Margaret, trained at the Slade School of Art and was by all accounts a gifted wood carver who went on to become an honorary director of the Whitworth Gallery in Manchester. The house is now sub-divided into luxury apartments and, having visited one of these some years ago at the invitation of a friend who was renting one on a twelve-month lease, I can tell you the position is wondrous and the views sublime. The families that lived 'on the hill' included barristers, surgeons, textile barons and anyone who had the means to build and maintain such a grand house. To try and understand just what it was like to live in such splendour, you can do no better than read the excellent autobiography *Manchester Made Them*, written by Katherine Chorley, who grew up in the centre of this middle-class enclave. She tells how her own family employed a nanny, chauffeur/handyman, three gardeners and several house staff. It is written without pretention and gives a wonderful insight into a gentler age.

Onwards and upwards I stumbled, 'this bloody road is a nightmare', until I came to Underwood Road, which conveniently links back to Macclesfield Road. On the corner is the house of the same name. The one-time home of M S Bles, a prominent Jewish businessman of Dutch origin. From this fine red and cream brick house, Mr Bles and others would walk the half-mile or so down the steep hill to the railway station, their first-class rail-pass in the form of a silver coloured disc proudly displayed from their watch chains.

I was roughly half way up Woodbrook Road at this point, so on I pressed. It's peculiar how different things sound when you are not cocooned in a car. From my own crunching footsteps to the birdsong and the distant sound of a heavy lawnmower, as it perfected, I presumed, horizontal stripes across a sublime lawn – each sound seeming more acute, more alive. The hill seemed to go on forever but any physical discomfort was more than compensated for with these utterly distracting properties. Every so often I would catch a glimpse of an open gate, leading to a sublime villa, or stop to take in the sight of a lofty home perched at the head of a winding drive. A number of the villas leading back to the Macclesfield Road have reduced their huge land size and now have new mini mansions crafted carefully into the landscape, and very nice they look too. These will no doubt, become the homes of local footballers or similar – and Alderley Edge does what it has always done – moves on – not at breakneck speed leaving in its wake a series of planning disasters, but slowly and calmly.

The descent from the top of Macclesfield Road was a breeze; in fact so steep is this road that it was difficult to keep my pace to a walk, as every so often, I found myself breaking into a tiny-stepped trot, rather like those walkers you see in the Olympics who end up being disqualified for crossing what to me is an imperceptible line between walking and running. Within a very short time, I was sat outside Costa Coffee on the main street in Alderley Edge, sipping at a cappuccino and doing some serious damage to a blueberry muffin.

I parked the car in the National Trust car park at the 'Edge over Alderley' and shovelled too many coins into a greedy machine. What is it with the National Trust and their charges? Here we have a huge chunk of land, once owned by the Stanley family, who at least allowed free rambling on certain days of the year. Then, when in 1938 Alderley Park – the Stanley's ancestral home – became crippled with double death duties, the Pilkington sisters stepped in and bought 218 acres around Wizards Wood and the Edge for the people of Alderley, they too allowed free access. In 1948 they gifted the whole in memory of their parents to the National Trust – who, despite not paying a penny for the land, and I presume no rates, skin the arse off everybody with these bloody green robots. The sheer volume of money I had transferred to the National Trust's coffers during the past few months made me realise I should have paid the £40 membership fee. Although I don't feel quite of an age to be donning the pale green badge. Once embedded on their mailing list, I would be inundated with all those offers for boot-scrapers and tea towels. I know I wouldn't be able to resist such temptation. My cupboards would gradually swell under the weight of NT goodies – far cheaper to put the coins in the machine and go and visit the Edge.

My fellow walkers on the Edge this bright and breezy afternoon were an eclectic mix of green-wellied, Barbour-jacketed fifty-somethings taking Rover, or in one case Gerald, for walkies, serious ramblers with stout boots, trousers rolled into thick comfy socks (why do they do that?), younger girls and boys, totally prepared for every weather condition and eventuality by dressing in jeans, cotton tops and trainers. Then there was me, somewhere in between. I donned a pair of chunky-soled shoes, jeans and, despite the warm weather, I had included a light jumper in my survival pack.

The Edge over Alderley is old – in fact it is ancient. There are records to show that the Romans, Celts and Saxons all considered the Edge to be of importance. It has always had strong mystical associations – and as recently as 1960, it was known to be a regular meeting spot for at least one coven. The name is believed to be derived from the Alder tree, at one time held sacred in northern England.

As if to prove to prove the point – you should never judge a book by its cover – an elderly couple, who at first sight appeared as though they would be incapable of tying up their stout shoes never mind hiking, were now yomping on ahead of me like a couple of ex-marines. With the aid of stout sticks and buried under matching tweed plant-pot hats (this, despite the temperature now hitting a very pleasant 22 or so). Perhaps they knew something about the rapid change in conditions around these parts?

It was nice to be on the Edge again – so to speak. Although I live no more than a ten minute car drive from this beauty spot, I couldn't actually recall the last time I had visited it. One thing I had forgotten, was just how many dogs are let off their leash around these parts. I have nothing against dogs as such, but they obviously don't think the same about me – and some of these dogs were huge. Maybe this is why I'd taken so long to return?

In addition to the witches, there is also an ancient legend attached to the Edge. It is believed to be King Arthur's hiding place as he waits for the day of his 'needed return'.

This is how the legend goes:

> One autumn morning, a farmer was taking his beautiful white mare from his farm in Mobberley to the market in Macclesfield, via way of the Edge. Upon passing Thieves' Hole the horse stopped abruptly and refused to move. Then out of nowhere there appeared an old man with long hair and a flowing beard, dressed in a dark full length robe. The old man offered to buy the horse from the farmer, but he flatly refused, saying he would receive a better price at the market.
> "Then go," said the old man, "but remember this, your horse will be much admired, but no buyer will come forth and I will await your return, then you will sell the mare to me."

The horse was indeed, as the old man had predicted, 'much admired' but no buyer came forth. Trudging home across the Edge the farmer reached Thieves' Hole. Once again he was confronted by a man, although this time he was not an old man but an erect, proud wizard holding a staff in his right hand. The wizard led both the farmer and his horse past Seven Firs, the Golden Stone, Stormy Point and Saddlebole until he reached a large rock embedded in the hillside.

The wizard tapped the rock with his staff and the rock split in two, revealing a pair of Iron Gates. The farmer fell to his knees begging for mercy. The wizard told the farmer he shouldn't be afraid and beckoned both the man and his horse through a narrow cave and into a large cavern full of sleeping knights. Beside all but one knight was a white mare. The wizard then led the farmer into another cavern full of jewels and told him to take his share as payment for the horse. He then went on to explain that 'in a future time, within the reign of George, son of George (you don't think he meant Bush, do you?), these knights will awake and fight a decisive battle on the plain below, which will save the country'.

The wizard told the astonished farmer to leave, and the iron gates slammed firmly behind him. The farmer returned on many occasions and tried to find the Iron Gates, but to no avail.

I trudged on along a narrowing path and suddenly realised my feet were becoming heavier, or to be precise, my shoes were. The firm path had now turned into a cloggy mud route, obviously still sodden from the previous week's rain, the heavily wooded area receiving little benefit from the sun's warming rays. With shoes that were rapidly turning into those worn by Frankenstein's monster, I searched in vain for some way to scrape away the offending glug. Stood on one leg and leaning against a tree, I was attempting this delicate manoeuvre, when around the bend bounced the beast and, the following moment, a distant voice called out, "Nelson, Nelson, come here, come boy."

Up bounded Nelson and stopped a mere two feet or so away from me, tail wagging, tongue panting, and paws the size of dinner plates.

"Don't even think of jumping up at me with those muddy paws."

I'm not good on breeds of dogs: he was obviously a cross – somewhere between a Golden Labrador and a donkey at a guess. Why Nelson, I wondered? He wasn't pale with a dark patch around one eye, he wasn't minus one leg and certainly wasn't an 'Admirable Dog', sorry.

Nelson and I stood in resolute gaze upon each other until the impasse was broken, as his equally bulky owner hove into view, cane in one hand (I wish I had) and lead in the other.

"Soft as a brush, he only wants you to pat him," said his owner.

I smiled and declined. Why is it that dog owners have a completely different viewpoint to the rest of us about their beloved pets? I presume had he come across Nelson with his teeth firmly embedded in my thigh, his stock answer would have been... "Strange, he doesn't normally do that."

Four inches shorter after removing the half-a-hundredweight of mud from my shoes, I progressed towards the Edge. The pathway was now a carpet of soggy leaves as I dodged huge puddles and thick sticky mud. Dappled sunlight tried its best to break through dark woods and heavy foliage, but to little effect. All my fellow walkers had dispersed in different directions and I was left eerily alone. I only hope I'm not confronted by a man with a flowing beard in search of another white mare. I was beginning to see why the old farmer felt somewhat threatened.

Another fifteen minutes of hard walking, and I came to a clearing in the woods and a steep path which led to a rocky outpost. Sliding involuntarily to the bottom of the path, I looked for all the world as though I was snow-boarding - but without the board. Once on the sandstone plateau, the whole of the Cheshire plain lay before me like an oversized postcard – it was beautiful. On a large stone-built pillar, was a metal plaque declaring that in 1948 the whole of the parkland known as the Edge had been gifted to the National Trust in memory of Ma and Pa Pilkington – those weren't the exact words.

The pathway from here onwards became more challenging, with precipitous drops and narrow ledges, that did not need a coating of mud and leaves to make them feel somewhat threatening. I stopped for a moment and tried to work out just where I was within the park. Then something struck me – throughout the whole time within this wooded area, I hadn't heard one single bird. I had been told this odd fact before by others who regularly walked these paths but only now, standing alone with no other sound, save for the gentle rustle of the trees, did this fact occur to me – odd !

The next landmark I stumbled upon was Beacon Point. I would like to say that I had planned my route and that this was my next intended stop. Unfortunately that wouldn't be true. I simply stumbled across it as I fumbled my way along identical routes. This is the highest point on the Edge, so became the ideal point for one of the 'Cheshire Beacons'. Believed to date from the mid-16th century, its use is noted along with Helsby and Frodsham in the east and Blackstone Edge in Yorkshire as a warning beacon for the Spanish Armada's approach – a sort of latter-day email. Originally a square building had stood on this spot. It gradually fell into disrepair and collapsed in a gale in 1931. All that remains is another stone-built block and a metal plaque.

Evidence of axe heads and course hammers found in the mid-19th century suggest that as early as the Bronze Age this area was being mined. Certainly by the Middle Ages Alderley was known to have rich deposits of copper ore and the Edge is littered with mine shafts and open caves, as this area was actively mined up until the early 20th century. Most of them are, thankfully, either fenced off or clearly marked. It would be easy to see the attraction to youngsters in venturing within these caves, but they have been documented by caving clubs and others as particularly difficult, as man-made openings suddenly link to natural deep-ridged caverns – no mention of sleeping knights though.

It was also easy to work out that the Edge was not a place to wander around after dark. There were mine shafts and uneven terrain aplenty, but one of the most worrying aspects of this park were the narrow paths that either came to an abrupt end or were pitched at such an angle that, unless you had one leg four inches shorter than the other, you were in deep trouble. The other thing conspicuous by their absence was the lack of signs. Health and Safety would have a ball set free upon the Edge.

Still not exactly sure of my bearings, I proceeded along narrow paths and practically hacked my way through deep foliage until I suddenly came across a clearing with yet another huge sandstone ridge, and a view so arresting that I was drawn without fear towards the edge of the huge sandstone outpost. Completely unaware of any danger, I casually looked down. I was, without any warning, standing on the edge of a forty foot drop.

Visibly shaken, I slowly pulled away. I had been literally one step away from nose-diving to, if not sudden death, then certainly a thumping headache. If they ever decide to place any signage on the Edge, this place should have a bloody great STOP sign – it really is very dangerous! Still feeling somewhat shaken, I returned to my car before my allotted time ran out and I had to make another donation to the NT.

Sat at a table in Gusto, an Italian restaurant in Alderley Edge, I watched as the boys and girls packed the front bar, while others waited patiently for a much coveted table – it really does get busy after 7pm. This time I was with my wife Carolyn and my son Edward. I could think of no nicer place to be on a summer's evening and no better way to end my journey. I had set out several months ago to prove that life does exist in the middle and outer reaches of the North. I had, on reflection, been remiss in my appreciation of so many things. The beauty of North Yorkshire, with its wonderful sleepy villages and untouched landscapes. The stoic enthusiasm of the Geordie people, who seem capable of smiling whatever fate throws their way – and my goodness, fate has certainly done that over the years. The wistful beauty of Holy Island and the timeless appeal of the Lake District, not to mention the areas so close to my home that I had simply neglected to visit or, like the Edge, revisit. I had met characters aplenty and found kindness in the many small acts that people freely carried out to help me on my way. The transport and travel had been relatively easy and even the weather despite an inglorious late summer had been, on the whole, kind to me.

So next time you are thinking of taking a trip in the UK, why not set your compass or sat-nav to North, and come and see what you're missing... NORTH OF WATFORD GAP.

A special thanks to the following people and organisations:

The John Rylands Library, Deansgate, Manchester.

The Museum of Science & Industry, Manchester.

The Emmeline Pankhurst Centre, Nelson Street, Manchester.

The staff of Manchester Town Hall.

Fitzpatrick's Temperance Bar, Rawtenstall, Lancashire.

The Haworth Art Gallery, Accrington, Lancashire.

Brian & The Worth Valley Railway

Jill & Tom Wilson – The Helaina Hotel, 14 Blenheim Terrace, Scarborough, Norh Yorkshire.

Tricolos, 36–38 Newborough, Scarborough, North Yorkshire.

The staff of St Mary's Church, Whitby, North Yorkshire.

Hillary – Hexham Old Gaol, Hexham, Northumberland.

The Midland Hotel, Morecambe, Lancashire.

Dave Roscoe & The Williamson Tunnels, Smithdown Road Liverpool.

For more information and photos of the places featured within
this book please visit www.northofwatfordgap.co.uk